Memories of West Wicklow

T0345582

CLASSICS OF IRISH HISTORY

General Editor: Tom Garvin

Original publication dates of reprinted titles are given in brackets

Memories of West Wicklow

1813–1939

WILLIAM HANBIDGE &
MARY ANN HANBIDGE

edited and introduced by
W. J. Mc Cormack

from an edition privately published
by Mary Ann Hanbidge

UNIVERSITY COLLEGE DUBLIN PRESS
Preas Choláiste Ollscoile Bhaile Átha Cliath

First published by Mary Ann Hanbidge, 1939
This edition first published by University College Dublin Press, 2005
© W. J. Mc Cormack, 2005

ISBN 1-904558-24-0
ISSN 1393-6883

University College Dublin Press
Newman House, 86 St Stephen's Green
Dublin 2, Ireland

Cataloguing in Publication data available from the British Library

Typeset in Ireland in Ehrhardt by
Elaine Burberry, Bantry, Co. Cork
Text design by Lyn Davies
Printed on acid-free paper in Ireland by ColourBooks, Dublin

CONTENTS

William Hanbridge

FROM SWIFT TO 'THE DEAD'

W. J. Mc Cormack

I INTRODUCING WILLIAM HANBIDGE OF WICKLOW

The parishes of Dunlavin and Donoughmore lie at the western base of the Wicklow Mountains. Their position is rendered anomalous by the easy access they enjoy to counties Kildare (further west) and Dublin (to the north) compared with their social distance from the eastern portion of County Wicklow beyond the mountains (where I spent much of my childhood). Despite their adjacency, the two parishes differ essentially in structure, Dunlavin based on an elegant village laid out with broad streets, Donoughmore an entirely rural though once populous district. (Donard intervenes between them.) The area generally is sequestered, and was even more so in the early nineteenth century when William Hanbidge was born in the townland of Tinnahinch, parish of Donoughmore.

The great upheaval of recent years had been the insurrection of 1798 under the leadership of the United Irishmen. Government broke the rebel advance at the Battle of Arklow on 9 June, preventing the Wexford men from linking up with their comrades in Wicklow and Dublin. But resistance was maintained in much of County Wicklow, principally due to the efforts of two men – Michael Dwyer (1771–1826) and Joseph Holt (1756–1826). One valuable element in Hanbidge's recollections is his occasional reference to Dwyer's career. One oddly missing element is any reference to Holt.[1]

As a popular movement, the United Irishman rebellion in Leinster was largely confined to Wexford and did not outlast the crucial agricultural cycle from haymaking to winter planting. Consequently, in Wicklow there was little ensuing disruption to the rural economy and way of life (as occurred in the Vendée of western France for example), once the immediate conflicts were over. Of these the most important was the unauthorised execution in Dunlavin village of 34 or so prisoners in late May 1798. The perpetrators of this outrage were County Wicklow militiamen, who were loyalist and Protestant enthusiasts. The victims were local craftsmen or labourers. A broadsheet ballad quickly established the notoriety of the event in folk memory:

> Bad luck to you, Saunders, for you did their lives betray;
> You said a parade would be held on that very day,
> Our drums did rattle – our fifes did sweetly play;
> Surrounded we were and privately marched away.[2]

Like the Holts, the Hanbidges belonged to the Protestant Church of Ireland. These families were not, however, part of the ruling and landowning class, for they occupied far humbler stations in the politico-social system. Joseph Holt, who came from the eastern side of the Mountains, was a strong-minded, assertive individual, whereas the Hanbidge style was compliant, dutiful and sober.

1   See Peter O'Shaughnessy (ed.), *Rebellion in Wicklow: General Joseph Holt's Personal Account of 1798* (Dublin: Four Courts, 1998). Holt's memoirs included further material describing his life in the penal colonies in Australia, from which he was eventually released to return to Ireland.

2   Colm O Lochlainn, *Irish Street Ballads* (Dublin: Three Candles, 1939), pp. 106–7; see also Chris Lawlor, *The Massacre on Dunlavin Green: A Story of the 1798 Rebellion* (n.p., 1998).

Having risen to be a trusted employee of the county, Holt fell foul of the newly established Orange Order and of his own ambitious landlord. Propelled into rebellion by assaults on his property, and by his own forceful character, he quickly became a guerilla leader of exceptional ability, surrendering on terms favourable to his own survival. Although a native and resident of the Roundwood area, Holt held the central mountains during his campaign and linked up with Dwyer's West Wicklow contingent. To some extent he enjoyed the sympathy or protection of the Synge family who, through alliances with the Hutchinsons, were represented on both sides of the Wicklow Mountains.[3] Mary Ann Hanbidge (1866–1951), first editor of these *Memories*, notes the benefactions of Sir Samuel Synge Hutchinson during the local famine of 1817 when her father was four years old.

Born in 1813 William Hanbidge heard tales of '98 in his childhood. Though he acquired sufficient education to become in time a teacher, he makes no reference to Holt's *Memoirs* (a bowdlerised version appeared in 1838) or to Mary Leadbeater's more reliable account (published 1862) of conditions in West Wicklow. Her family was Quaker, based at Ballitore, a village in County Kildare some eight miles from Dunlavin.[4] Writing in his extreme old age, after the centenary of 1798 had been celebrated and counter-celebrated, Hanbidge was not concerned to place his memoir in any interpretive context as far as the Rebellion was concerned. Nevertheless, the events of 1798 affected the lives of his generation and social constituency in many regards. Even today, a member of the family can explain William's neglect of Holt to the advantage of Dwyer,

3   On the Synges in East and West Wicklow, see W. J. Mc Cormack, *The Silence of Barbara Synge* (Manchester: Manchester University Press), 2003.

4   Mary Leadbeater, *The Annals of Ballitore, with a Memoir of the Author, Letters from Edmund Burke heretofore Unpublished, and the Correspondence of Mrs R. Trench and the Rev George Crabbe* (London: Bell & Daldy, 1862).

not by reference to religious affiliation, but by pointing out that the latter was 'a local'.

Towards the end of his *Memories*, William Hanbidge makes two apparently disjointed observations one after the other:

> The Protestants of Donough [*sic*] had but little intercourse with their Romanist neighbours (my brothers had not) but one day I remember a meeting.

> The first Hanbidges who [*sic*] came to Ireland with I think William the third prince of Orange and there have been Orangemen in their family from that time to this. I myself was secretary to an Orange lodge and attended orange lodges in London some years ago.

In the connection with the second of these, the claim of arrival in Ireland in the late seventeenth century is evidently correct, though the closeness to King William has perhaps been exaggerated. The Hanbidges came from Gloucester, where they were an established trade family.[5] They were not Huguenots, as is sometimes supposed. A certain awkwardness in the phrases just quoted derives from the author's old age, his limited formal education, and indeed his deliberately plain literary style. However, the two or three little sentences also convey the constricted social circumstances of the family in early nineteenth-century West Wicklow and the manner in which ideological associations were carried over into metropoli-tan life.[6] The formation of the Orange Order in 1795 had contributed

5   In the edition of 1939, Mary Hanbidge reproduces great quantities of evidence relating to Hanbidges in Gloucester, from which it is clear the Irish family results.

6   These sentences are to be found in 'Appendix C', the four-page document printed by Mary Hanbidge after the volume proper had been completed: from her style of presentation it is not wholly clear whether her father wrote them sequentially or whether perhaps she has brought them into the order in which they appear. Not every copy of the 1939 volume contains Appendix C, even among those distributed to family members in

mightily to the crisis which broke three years later, and Wicklow
was one of the earliest counties to be organised by the Order.
Deliberately or otherwise, Hanbidge obscures the issue of his
family's relationship with Orangeism at the time of the Rebellion and
its suppression, replacing it with a double perspective. Accordingly,
'Orangemen' enjoy an undifferentiated existence from the days of
King Billy right through to the present. Meanwhile the author's
own engagement with them is displaced from Wicklow to Victorian
London where the matter was of lesser weight. Stylistically, one
should note that he refers in these sentences to the Hanbidges and
'their [*sic*] family', as if he were not writing about his own father and
uncles, indeed about himself. The plain style, so central to notions
of puritan narrative and reflection, has its own cunning passages.

Hanbidge's view of history is inevitably and unremarkably
bounded by the Protestant succession guaranteed by William of
Orange through four decisive battles fought against Jacobite forces
at 'Derry, Aughrim, Enniskillen and the Boyne'. While Dunlavin
and Donoughmore were remote from these sites of epochal change,
they were quickly inscribed into the ecclesiastical annals of Glorious
Revolution. Jonathan Swift (1667–1745) sat in the prebendal stalls
of St Patrick's Cathedral, Dublin, as rector of Dunlavin, and his
income from this source contributed significantly to the stabilisation
of his financial affairs.[7] The neighbouring parish of Donoughmore –
though more remote in its location – also filled a prebendal stall in
the Cathedral, a notable occupant in the 1720s being Francis Corbett
or Corbet (1688–1775), treasurer of St Patrick's. For such eminences,

West Wicklow. My own copy, formerly the property of the North London Collegiate
School (which Mary Ann Hanbidge had attended as a pupil) and purchased second-hand
in Dublin, does contain it, loose. Appendix C is included in this edition as 'Matters not
printed in the main body of 'Memories', on pp. 76–80.

7   See Irvin Ehrenpreis, *Swift: the Man, his Works and the Age: Vol. 2, Dr Swift* (London:
Methuen, 1967), p. 13.

parochial duties were virtually non-existent, the work falling to a curate. Writing of Donoughmore as it was a century later, Hanbidge describes the collapse of this devolved responsibility with the growth of a more lively religious sensibility after 1800. The clerical agent of the change is the Reverend Mr Thomas Francis Greene, curate to a succession of rectors, but his younger lay equivalent is the author himself, William Hanbidge.

Though Swift and Corbett may never have set foot in Hanbidge's native place, the continuing links with Patrick's Cathedral put Dunlavin and Donoughmore in contact with the capital to a degree transcending the parish's geographical obscurity. Among those neighbours with whom Hanbidges intermarried one notes the name Molyneux (variously spelled) as further evidence of a slow traffic between notable Dublin citizen-families and rural outposts. Sir Samuel Synge Hutchinson (1756–1846), at his seat in Castle Sallagh, was brother to the former MP for Swords just north of Dublin, Francis Synge (1761–1831), great-grandfather of the dramatist, J. M. Synge (1871–1909). Synges were intermarried with Hatches, and one John Hatch was long and lucratively Seneschal of Saint Sepulchre's, an ecclesiastical property associated with the Cathedral. A younger Dr John Hatch served as a churchwarden in Dunlavin during the period when William Hanbidge was training as a teacher.[8] Social mobility in another direction is exemplified in the Cramptons who, in addition to intermarrying with Hanbidges, provided the city of Dublin with one of its premier firms of house-builders, G & T Crampton Ltd.

The Swift whose name features in the records of Dunlavin parish is not reducible to an office-holder in the Cathedral. He is the author of *Gulliver's Travels*, a master of English prose fiction

---

8   For an account of Dr Hatch's career in Dunlavin and (later) in Annamoe, see Mc Cormack, *The Silence of Barbara Synge*, pp. 186–93.

in a tradition reaching back through the puritans to Elizabethan experiments with the novel. He is also author of that more urgent, contemporary and anonymous writing, *A Modest Proposal for Preventing the Children of Poor People from Being a Burthen to their Parents or the Country, and for Making Them Beneficial to the Public* (1729). Among the measures adopted in response to the scandalous poverty publicised by Swift was the establishment of Charter Schools throughout the country. With time, these became almost as scandalous in their treatment of children as the proposal ironically made by the dean of St Patrick's.

Hanbidge's admission to the Kildare Place Training School may well have been assisted by contact with influential figures in the parish, several of whom were connected to the Cathedral through the prebendal stalls and otherwise. Hanbidge recalls that he was taught arithmetic by the Pestalozzian method, just then introduced into Ireland by John Synge (1788–1845), son of the MP, and master of Roundwood (later of Glanmore also) on the other side of the Wicklow Mountains. By 1829, the Kildare Place schools were embroiled in sectarian controversy, fuelled by resistance to Daniel O'Connell's campaign for Catholic Emancipation. What had been intended as an integrated primary educational system became one side of a battle for control of religious instruction. Hanbidge's recollections characteristically play down the element of conflict though – again in his plain respect for fact – he discloses a relationship between Kildare Place and the Foundling Hospital which may have advanced him towards a teaching career. As a child, he had been instructed in scripture 'by a girl named Eliza Styles whom the schoolmaster got as an app[r]entice out of the Foundling hospital [in] James St. Dublin'. Later, when he went up to Dublin he found himself immured in classes 'held in a house on the premises of the Foundling hospital where we never were allowed out into the streets unless on Sunday[s] afternoons and not then if we had not

given satisfaction in our studies the previous week.' Annotating the
Memories in the late 1930s, Hanbidge's daughter questioned
whether this was in fact the Kildare Place training school and not
some other establishment dedicated to the same purpose. One way
or the other, her father's education, both as a child and as a trainee
teacher, was touched by Dublin's prolific Foundling Hospital.

This institution had become subject to a parliamentary Committee
of Enquiry early in the 1790s. The ensuing report provided damning
statistics about the practice of farming out virtual infants, especially
to the area round Dunlavin: of more than 460 children placed with
families there, only 65 could be reliably traced a few years later. If
prebendal stalls provided the high road between capital and cottage,
the Foundling Hospital laid down a darker and lower trail of
sorrow. Things had probably improved by the time young William
Hanbidge was coming to consciousness, but this was in part due to
government's insistence that vacant posts in certain charity schools
be filled from the ranks of the Hospital's older pupils – Eliza Styles
was almost certainly one of these.[9] The Carlow/Wicklow/Dublin
border-areas were particularly favoured by the Hospital authorities
for the farming out of surplus children; Dunlavin was sufficiently
central in this well-established practice to warrant special treatment
in the official Enquiry. The background to Hanbidge's earliest
recollections was thus coloured and shaped by a variety of powerful
influences, with the Rebellion serving only as the most obvious.

As the nineteenth century unfolded, West Wicklow felt the
pressure of disasters occurring on a national scale. The Famine of
1845–7 struck the south and west of the country with particular
ferocity. Hanbidge's account of a visit to County Cork does not vie
with the outraged rhetoric of John Mitchel or the later and more
intimate recollections of Father Peter O'Leary in *Mo Sgéal Féin*

9   Kenneth Milne, *The Irish Charter Schools 1730–1830* (Dublin: Four Courts, 1997), p. 266.

(1915). As with 1798, the Great Famine was a historical topic by 1900 as well as a historical event. His recollections are largely focused on charitable work undertaken in Ireland and in New York; again an irenic, or ecumenical, perspective is adopted as he notes with approval the promptness with which the Catholic boys in his charge were taken into care by priests, and chides the memory of Episcopalian and Wesleyan ministers of whom he saw little. These paragraphs are noteworthy, however, more for their asides than their substance – the good meal eaten in a Cork hotel amidst famine, the filth of Bandon (where, legend has it, in those days even the pigs were Protestant), the killing of a shark on board the *Finland*, the class of New York black boys whom he taught one Sunday, and so forth. The auspices he had conveyed his charges under were those of the Evangelical Protestant Alliance, evidently eschewing the proselytism so often ascribed to famine relief work. While in the vicinity of Schull in West Cork, Hanbidge very likely met the rector, Robert Traill, whose daughter married John Hatch Synge (1823–72) and became the playwright's mother in 1871. Traill railed against Catholicism, but laboured unto the death to assist all his parishioners in distress, likewise without recourse to spiritual extortion.

Referring to Frederick Eyre Trench (died 1848) as rector of Cloughjordan in Tipperary, Hanbidge passes over a closer relationship – his reverence was rector-prebend of Dunlavin from mid-1819 till death. Cloughjordan, however, lay close to the Trench family estate, where F. E. Trench conducted a local school under the auspices of the London Hibernian Society, a somewhat friendly rival of the Kildare Place endeavour. Largely an absentee from West Wicklow (Mr Greene did the honours), Trench contributed to the moral economy of his own inheritance by the instruction given, or at least proposed, in the school. A pious English aristocratic and Baptist visitor in the 1830s sympathetically described the poverty of Irish labourers in general, the indifference of the upper classes and many Established Church clergy, and the crude discipline imposed by 'Romish' priests. Of Trench's school he wrote:

> There are about thirty children present, of whom scarcely any were Roman Catholics. Children of that creed had attended, but the priest had established in the neighbourhood a rival school, to which he had drawn nearly all of them. It is obvious that this policy may be effectual through all Ireland, if Protestant schools are conducted unintelligently. Nor need the remark be confined to Ireland. Nothing is scarcely more important to the empire than that the education of the young should be in the hands of religious persons.[10]

It would be a mistake to assume that Hanbidge held the same views as far as Ireland was concerned. His memories have their odd gaps and silences. As an Irishman recently settled in Hoxton, he cannot have missed the Fenian explosion at Clerkenwell Jail in December 1867, or the last public execution at Newgate, which resulted. The absence of condemnation, or even comment, may stem from charity. In contrast, his later disgust with William Ewart Gladstone and what he strongly terms the Prime Minister's 'ignoble' South African policy is incisively recorded.

By 1881, Hanbidge was well established in London, yet evidently attached by strong feeling to his native place. The most striking absence from these pages is any reference to the most famous Wicklow man of the day, Charles Stewart Parnell (1846–1891). The word 'home' recurs with almost liturgical fidelity in the *Memories*, but it is never contaminated with any allusion to the quest for Home Rule in Ireland. Despite a rumbling constitutional crisis throughout the 1880s, and the traumatic circumstances of Parnell's fall from power and sudden death, none of this political matter impinges on Hanbidge or at least on the record of his memories and concerns.

10   The Hon. Wriothesley Noel, *Notes of a Short Tour Through the Midland Counties of Ireland in the Summer of 1836* (London, 1837).

Evangelicals frequently distanced themselves from political affairs – except in Ulster – regarding them as 'of the world'. Distanced from his fellow-Anglican Parnell, Hanbidge nevertheless chastised Gladstone, a saint to some among nonconformist voters. Again, his age must be taken into account in assessing the completeness of what was undertaken as a brief *résumé* of his life, especially his youth. As he makes clear, when he believed he had fulfilled his undertaking to write, he decided simply to continue, adding new material without any revision of what had gone before. A third stage, headed 'A Few Anecdotes of the Irish Rebellion of 1798 as I Heard From My Father', takes the reader back not only to the author's earliest days but to those formative and violent experiences which preceded his birth. A naïve approach to narrative may be suspected, but there is a profound aptness in the shape of the *Memories* as they reach us. Instead of any embroilment in recent controversies, any enflaming of Parnellite and anti-Parnellite emotions, Hanbidge substitutes brief comments on matters which were even more traumatic in their time but which have acquired a suture of antiquarian recovery.

In fact, the tripartite narrative has not quite closed. There still remain 'Matters not printed in the main body of "Memories" for various reasons: religious, political or personal'. Here one clearly discerns the influence, if not indeed the hand, of Hanbidge's daughter who prepared the text for publication in 1939: these 'Matters' were printed up on a single sheet of paper, separately paginated from the book proper and circulated loose, perhaps only to approved buyers/readers.[11] This was a fraught moment, locally

11 *The Memories of William Hanbidge Aged 93. 1906. An Autobiography with Appendices and Chronicles of his Family by his Daughter Mary Hanbidge. For Private Circulation Only.* St Albans: [printed by] Gibbs & Bamforth Ltd, 1939. 308 pp. with (in some copies) a single sheet insert 'Appendix C'. A note dated Remembrance Day [i.e. 11 November 1939] on p. 306 states that war had delayed printing of the book.

and internationally. The Glen of Imaal, which looms over the
Hanbidge acres, had been a place of refuge for Holt and Dwyer after
1798; under an independent Irish government, it was now used by
the national army as an artillery firing range. Despite the presence
of Mr de Valera's uniformed soldiers, the empty vastness of West
Wicklow provided cover for many an enemy of the state, IRA men
on the run or in training. Hanbidge's last additional material
concludes with a strangely intimate detail from 1798:

> A wounded rebel took refuge with a Mrs Valentine at the entrance to
> Saunders' Grove who was loved by Mrs Valentine who proposed to
> elope with him, but as he had a sweetheart he refused so in refenge [*sic*]
> she informed on him when he was taken and shot. A few nights
> afterwards she was fearfully mutulated [*sic*] and murdered.[12]

Morley Saunders it was who had trapped his humble neighbours, confined them, and so virtually signed their death warrants
on Dunlavin Green, despite having been a liberal landlord in the
years running up to the Insurrection. Memories lived long in such
a district, names were recalled with affection or loathing. Among
the minor figures whom William Hanbidge mentions are Peter
Plant, Black Jem Plant, and a Mrs Plant who was sextoness at the
church in Donoughmore. His editor-daughter adds an extensive
footnote, establishing that the Plant family had loyally filled that
office from 1818 until 1910. (At least one member of the family was
living in the parish in 1938, and the two families had intermarried
at least once.) Her motives in doing so went beyond scholarly zeal:
in the late 1930s, two Plant brothers (nominally Protestants) were
notorious as IRA men specialising in bank-robbery and (in the case

---

12   From Mary Hanbidge's notes, it emerges that Hanbidges and Valentines were related
by marriage, though the alliance post-dated 1798.

of George Plant, 1904–42) in summary execution of dissident fellow-republicans.[13] Thus while the erring Mrs Valentine of 1798 is accommodated in a discreet appendix, the good reputation of the Plants is diligently established – 'men and women shared in the work of the Church'. George Plant was executed by firing squad under military law in 1942 at Portlaoise Prison.

Memories of West Wicklow can only be read as a complex document, with the plain-style narrative of its author providing the principal but not the exclusive structuring element. In William Hanbidge's terms, it is the record of a long life devoted to what he would have called 'Bible Christianity'. The locus for his extensive labours in this cause is London, whence he travelled in 1858. Pastoral care best describes his activities which included elementary teaching, preaching the Gospel, and taking care of the vulnerable poor. The East End places which he names are almost as numerous as the townlands of West Wicklow, but with the former there is also a shortlist of organisations through which Hanbidge worked, notably the inter-denominational London City Mission. In secular terms, this is the world of Henry Mayhew (1812–87) whose *London Labour and the London Poor* had appeared in four volumes between 1851 and 1862. Victorian London was, in its own way, a feature of post-Famine Ireland, a non-land of plenty, cut off from the natural cycle of harvest and sowing, a sump of immiseration, capital of a kingdom derisively United.

In spirit, Hanbidge is closer to William Booth (1829–1912), founder of a slum mission in Whitechapel (1865) and of the

---

13 For a lengthy account of George Plant, see Michael Moroney, 'George Plant and the rule of law: The Devereux case (1940–1942)', *Journal of the Tipperary Historical Society* (1988); for two literary allusions to his fate, see 'The Last Republicans' in Austin Clarke, *Selected Poems* (London: Penguin, 1992) pp. 71–2, 225, and the more hermetic 'Quinta del Sordo' in Hugh Maxton, *Jubilee for Renegades* (Gerrards Cross: Colin Smythe, 1982).

Salvation Army (1877). The conventional churches' distaste for Booth's ragged and smelly converts is the background to Hanbidge's unsung Christian endeavour. Effortlessly articulate where the Dunlavin man was tongue-biting, Dublin's Bernard Shaw will follow Hanbidge into the Empire's lower depths, preaching a message superficially different but still founded on an ethic of work and a puritan contempt for mere happiness. Brick Lane, which was the equator of Hanbidge's mission-field, became in the 1930s a No Man's Land of street-warfare between Oswald Mosley's Union of Fascists and those Jews and others (mainly immigrants) who maintained their close East End communities. Hanbidge's rapport with Jewish neighbours is one of the most touching details in his little autobiography.

Mary Hanbidge, arranging these pages for the printer in late 1939, was motivated principally by a deep filial love of her dead father. Her extensive notes and genealogical trees testify to much else besides. She had become a successful head-school-mistress, an able administrator and researcher. Thus the ancillary material appearing in her decidedly prolix edition indirectly illuminates a second dimension to her father's *Memories*. While the plain-style narrative touched on inter-communal strife, the editorial matter aimed to bring out the theme of reconciliation. This involves a dialectical inversion of soul and body, itself a puritan rhetorical strategy of ancient provenance. Young Billy Hanbidge's physicality is unmistakable – the fights, the food, the hunger for female company. Some of his most affective descriptions of childhood relate to eating – the utensils used, and the range of the ordinary household's diet. Remarriage on two occasions confirms his bodily vigour. Even in old age and in London, he retained a physical strength to match his ardent spirit. In a dangerous crowd at a royal occasion in 1871, he pushed while his wife prayed. Nevertheless, on a larger register these elements of his story require careful treatment, especially as it is prepared for readers about to plunge into world war. Mary Hanbidge goes to great trouble to weave an acceptance of the new Irish state into her accompanying account of the farm at Tinnahinch. She cites Liam Price, a district court judge learned in local topography and (as it happens) a fellow-Protestant.[14] She acknowledges the assistance of various officials in government bodies, and alludes pointedly to the Gaelic language, thus signalling a tolerance of new orthodoxies in the land of her ancestors. Among the few words of Gaelic which she attributes to her father is *scailtín*, a form of hot punch made with whiskey and butter. There is no fulmination against Irish neutrality in the coming war and no arguing about the Treaty Ports, though pride in her late brother, Lieutenant-Colonel Robert William Hanbidge (1851–1936) is manifest. Elizabeth Bowen's wartime observation that neutrality for the Irish state amounted to a true religious principle deserves to be taken more seriously than calumniators of that novelist permit.

Between these two lines of mutual interpretation – the narrative and the annotative – *Memories* carries a third burthen. This is human reproduction. William Hanbidge married three times. His little book provides details of his own progeny (nine children) and that of his many siblings. For men without independent means, remarriage was not an unusual means of sustaining a household, allowing them to work while domestic matters (such as the children of a now dead wife) were taken care of. But Hanbidge is not just a manager of his affairs. He is unabashed in telling how, as a young man, he transferred his sexual interest from one young woman to another, before settling down to a life of serial monogamy punctuated by bereavement. In Appendix C, one of his brothers is plainly described as a 'libertine', while another is said to have abused mem-

---

14   See Christiaan Corlett and Mairéad Weaver (eds), *The Price Notebooks* 2 vols (Dublin: Dúchas, 2002).

bers of the family. His listing of dates of birth may be rudimental, but these illustrate the dominant economy of nineteenth-century Ireland, a Malthusian crisis of resources and demand. Unspecified financial pressures contributed to Hanbidge's departure to London, post-Famine Ireland being the depressed place it was. The megapolis presented him with a vision of human congestion, now urban whereas the overcrowding of Mayo and Cork had been rural. As the logic of Charles Dickens's fiction repeatedly demonstrates, there were too many people, too many mouths: bodies disappeared or dissolved, in orphanages, in sweat-factories, press-gangs, and the river. The dynamic linking Donoughmore to London was no better than the trail of sorrow winding out from the Foundling Hospital in Dublin's James Street. The author Hanbidge is in several regards a Dickensian character: his combination of humour and gentleness, his mental endurance and almost-visible bodily presence. If in these respects he recalls Wemmick of *Great Expectations* (serialised 1860–1), his language in the *Memories* is something Pip in the same novel weeps for, a *script*ure of honesty amid crass effulgence. When the idolised Prince Consort died in the year *Great Expectations* appeared in volume form, Hanbidge chose to preach to lodging-house dwellers on a text unlikely to please authority – 'A living dog is better than a dead lion' (Ecclesiastes 9: 4).

This resistance to ordained authority could be read as part of his puritan inheritance, were it not for another of the strange absences which mark the *Memories*. Nowhere can I trace the influence of *Pilgrim's Progress* (1678), that masterpiece of English prose litera-ture written partly in gaol by an unlicensed preacher. While the worldly William Makepeace Thackeray could take the title of his famous novel, *Vanity Fair* (1848), from John Bunyan's allegory, William Hanbidge inveighs against no Giant Despair nor points warningly to the Slough of Despond. Beyond this specific abstention, he does not treat the world as a place of pilgrimage, in which the faithful Christian must be ever vigilant. To be sure, faith is enjoined. But the word 'temptation' never occurs, though there are cautionary tales about drink, prostitution, and vice of every kind. Hanbidge is a decidedly modern figure, even if he seems unfashionably pious.

The dutiful listing of offspring is a conventional part of naive autobiography. In the case of a long-lived nineteenth-century Irishman, it is also a reinscription of the Famine as the central experience of the country's population, survivors at home as well as victims and emigrants. Human fertility contributed to unparalleled mortality, aided by harsh economic doctrine and indifferent government. Quite apart from the Famine's contribution to the growth of nationalism, and the related development of an Irish-American lobby, the experiences of Black '47 added to inter-church tensions in Ireland. Evangelicalism was associated with the tactic of offering soup in return for what amounted to apostasy. Theological distinctions which marked off one reformed church from another were simultaneously blurred, and the outcome was to render 'Protestant' indistinguishable from 'British' in many Irish Catholic eyes. At the same time in Britain, Irish Protestants were thought of as ferociously doctrinaire, big-game-hunters turned bestial in the wild. Hanbidge, for his part, is not averse to wagging the finger at drinking Catholics, or 'the dirty Irish'. As the political process gradually conceded successive degrees of participative democracy, the masses (or at least the male masses) became actively involved in electoral contests turning implicitly on these oppositions. The dissident Orangeman, William Johnston of Ballikilbeg, played this card as early as 1868, and set in motion a chain-reaction traceable even today. Again, one again notes Hanbidge's silence on the Home Rule crisis of 1885, unless his one allusion to an Orange Lodge meeting relates to this period.

Irish literature was not eloquent on the seismic upheavals of mid-to-late Victorian society. There is no Irish *Hard Times*, no

Irish equivalent of George Gissing's *Nether World* (1889), though
the materials were raw enough and accessible. Rural images per-
sisted: evictions attracted more attention than satanic mills. Among
the cities, Johnston's Belfast was peculiarly ignored. James Joyce
(1882–1941) broke certain moulds, not only in the urban realism of
Dubliners as a unified collection, but more specifically in 'Eveline'
and 'Counterparts' where northern accents and influences are heard
in the deposed capital. The urbanisation of fiction is no simple
desideratum in itself, like Marx's abolition of the village idiot.

In Joyce's final story, the rural West of Ireland returns like the
repressed to haunt reasonably affluent, anxiously reasonable Dublin.
It unfolds a pattern of vertiginous proportions. Mr Brown is
present as a far-from-representative Protestant, and the set-piece
description of Christmas bounty reveals itself as a parade ground of
intimidating military metaphors:

> In the centre of the table there stood, as sentries to a fruit-stand which
> upheld a pyramid of oranges and American apples, two squat old-
> fashioned decanters of cut glass, one containing port and the other dark
> sherry. On the closed square piano a pudding in a huge yellow dish lay
> in waiting, and behind it were three squads of bottles of stout and ale
> and minerals drawn up according to the colours of their uniforms, the
> first two black, with brown and red labels, the third and smallest squad
> white, with transverse green sashes.[15]

15 James Joyce, *Dubliners* (Harmondsworth: Penguin, 1962), p. 194. Military metaphor
occurs elsewhere in *Dubliners*, though not with such concentration; for an account of
'Eveline' in this regard, see W. J. Mc Cormack, *From Burke to Beckett: Ascendancy, Tradition
and Literary History* (Cork: Cork University Press, 1994), p. 262 etc. The account of 'The
Dead' synopsised above derives from a longer paper, delivered and lost at a conference in
University College Cork, the theme of which was Joyce's anatomising of the Irish Catholic
middle class as beneficiaries of the Famine. Evidence of the Famine's impact in Dublin
city supports this view. The pervasiveness of military metaphor in various discourses

Hanbidge's *Memories* came *ab ovo* with his description of cooked potatoes scooped out to serve as egg-cups. If collective eating is the occasion and place where symbolisation of culture is subordinated to its practice, then Joyce's story is as much a tribute to the bounty-hunter as to the agriculturalist. The violence upon which polite society is based, the uneasy security of a middle class which has survived the Famine and even thrived on the opportunities provided by reduced competition, is brilliantly reflected in the Morkans' cut glass. The musical activities of the night give way to unaccompanied storytelling. To be exact, Gabriel Conroy relates how old Patrick Morkan, who was a glue-boiler or ran a starch-mill, drove out with his horse – 'the never-to-be-forgotten Johnny' – to a military review in Phoenix Park. The unfortunate Johnny, accustomed to drudge in a circle all day driving the mill, felt compelled to circle endlessly round King William's statue when he saw that monument to the Glorious Revolution. This repeated story of repetitious conduct in deference to a real revolution replacing a formal review briefly threatens to re-impose the rule of sentries and uniformed squads.

One could stretch a point to suggest that Hanbidge's *Memories* resemble Gabriel's story or, more damaging, resemble the conduct of Patrick Morkan's horse. If the Never to be Forgotten Johnny could not pass the Immortal Memory, so William Hanbidge returns in his narrative to 1798, to the treachery or cowardice of Morley Saunders and the mutilation of Mrs Valentine. Instead of such formal closure, Joyce's story reaches its now-famous climax in the realisation of how the dead inform the living, that is, provide them with shape and form, purpose and dangerous information. The effect is to draw Gabriel towards vast hosts of the dead, away from the groaning board, the complacent singers, and well-heeled dancers.

during the first decade of the twentieth century is remarked on by Louis Bregar, *Freud: Darkness in the Midst of Vision* (New York: Wiley, 2000), pp. 191–3 etc. Indeed, classic psychoanalysis owes all too much to this imagery.

Patrick Morkan's career, upon which all this prosperity had been founded, flourished with the Famine. His manufactory recycled dead horses, making glue, unconvincingly euphemised as starch, stiffening, uprighteousness. His descendants, the accomplished but now ageing Misses Morkan, are the beneficiaries of decimation, rather starched in their collars and bodices. In the battle for life, they survived whereas the wretched figures seen in West Cork by William Hanbidge, William Le Fanu, Father Peter O'Leary, the Reverend Robert Traill and a dozen other witnesses, did not survive.

Have I removed William Hanbidge from all contexts of fair comparison by pitting him against the author of 'The Dead'? I do not think so. Among the witnesses shortlisted above, only he came from the soil, not – it should be admitted – from the lower depths, but from working stock, to observe the catastrophe of one county at a time of national catastrophe. His clipped observation – a good meal for the Reverend Trench, his agent, and the attendant Hanbidge, while wretches starve – has a Joycean economy. His neglect of Holt, the Fenians and Parnell exemplifies at a rudimentary level Stephen Dedalus's advice that, if we cannot change the country, let us at least change the subject. And his silence on Bunyan prompts one to ask how often Homer is mentioned in *Ulysses*?

II MARY ANN HANBIDGE OF LONDON

In fairness, William Hanbidge's editor/daughter deserves some extensive acknowledgement in these preliminary pages. In assessing her contribution to the present volume, we have to distinguish sharply between her career and her retirement. Born in London on 3 June 1866, she proved her academic abilities at a very early age. On the basis of successive scholarships, she advanced through local schools, a junior establishment in Kentish Town, and Bedford

College (a constituent of London University.) There she studied English literature and graduated BA, coming first place (according to her father's chronicle) in her year.

Given her straitened financial background, the choice of a career was urgent. She proceeded to the Cambridge Training College, the first residential seminary for would-be secondary teachers established in England. For six years she taught in St Helier, principal town of the Channel Islands, before moving back to the mainland and the prestigious and socially elevated Cheltenham Ladies' College. Already she had traversed a very diverse educational terrain, from the nonconformist (Congregational) infant schools, through the civic university (thought by some contemporaries a godless place) into one of the most fashionable secondary schools in the country. While there, she was able (in practice) to take leave, return to London and study for an MA at the University, after which she resumed duties in Cheltenham. Thus consolidated, a further move to the Central Foundation Girls School in the East End of London represented a descent on the social scale, at least as far as her pupils were the measure of this. But it was the Foundation School (founded in 1726 for the education of girls with no financial means) which became her professional home for life, as she was headmistress for more than thirty years, retiring in 1929.

Although Miss Hanbidge had encouraged her father to write up his recollections in 1906, it was only in the 1930s that she turned her attention to publishing them. Like many women of her generation, she had consciously or otherwise sacrificed marriage and family for the sake of her vocation as a teacher. She now turned back towards Ireland and West Wicklow, and began the research which culminated in the publication of 1939. All the political landmarks which her father would have recognised had disappeared, or had been so transformed as to be unrecognisable. Dublin was the capital

Mary Ann Hanbidge (1866–1951)

of a new state, still (to be sure) part of the British dominions but steadily manoeuvring to escape from the remaining formal links. In local terms, West Wicklow (where the British Army had maintained an artillery training camp) was undergoing the consequent adjustments with peculiar sensitivity. The Glen of Imaal had long been a distinctly Protestant district of small farmers, with a tradition of provendering the camp with hay, eggs and other agricultural produce. Horses were bought, and a brisk local economy was maintained. As with this commercial eclipse, coinciding with a general post-war depression, so displacement and replacement characterised other areas of social and political activitity. While the Free State settled down after the Civil War of 1922–3, the adherence of its conservative government to the social teaching of the Catholic Church became closer year by year.

Unlike barrack towns such as Fermoy or Sligo, West Wicklow did not experience any sudden exodus of families attached to, or serving, the departing military whose barracks in Imaal was more isolated than most country houses. Its pervasively agricultural character and dispersed population may have allowed for a gradual adjustment to the new regime. In addition, Wicklow had not featured prominently in the Civil War; rivalry between degrees of nationalism was muted, and the county emerged as one of the few returning a Labour Party deputy among its representatives in Dáil Éireann. It was to this relatively fortunate area of the new Ireland that Mary Hanbidge turned her attention.

If Dunlavin and Donoughmore were sequestered when her father had been born in 1813, links to the capital had improved considerably. The Bianconi road-coach by which she had travelled on her first visit in 1882 gave up the ghost to an expanding railway system within a few years. Stations were opened in Dunlavin and Baltinglass. Thus, Mary Hanbidge was able to move easily between her relatives in West Wicklow and the libraries of Dublin. It is not clear exactly when she determined to produce the austerely handsome volume which Gibbs & Bamforth of St Albans printed in 1939, but family tradition records that she decided all her resources would be channelled into the effort. Her surviving relatives would benefit little financially by her death, but she would ensure that each Hanbidge household would have its copy of the family history. A number of otherwise blank pages at the back, headed 'Family Notes', indicate a former headmistress's belief that her kin would continue to do their homework. Twenty-five plates bearing portrait photographs, reproductions of genealogical materials, and illustrations of sites associated with Hanbidges in England and Ireland, testify to her unstinting investment in the project.

In its large entirety, the 1939 volume suggests a division in the editor's sense of her own attachments in early old age. Her first concern is her father, and the accurate publication of his memories. These take pride of place in the opening pages, following by copious notes on the Wicklow Hanbidges, their successive smallholdings, interrelationships and progress in the world. But there follows a truly astonishing body of research devoted to the family's earlier origins in Gloucester, as if to suggest that the editor suspected that the English line might prove more permanent than the excursion to Wicklow, commenced in 1688 or thereabouts.

Ironically, it was West Wicklow which supplied the impetus for a third strand to Mary Hanbidge's research. Like most Irish families, individuals had emigrated at various points throughout the nineteenth-century. It was Kathleen Hanbidge (1900–81) of Brockna who put her English cousin in touch with some of the Canadian diaspora, a development which can be sensed in the somewhat breathless closing pages of the 1939 volume. Further assistance was provided by Sarah Hanbidge of Stratford-on-Slaney. Kathleen's daughter, Nora (born 1928), is the latest family historian, continuing the genealogies of 1939 in a locally produced book (1997) which has already run through two editions. As against an understated anxiety in the *Memories*, Nora Hanbidge reports that 'it is very gratifying to note that there are many more Hanbidge households in the Wicklow area than in 1939'. The railway line through West Wicklow prospered less under post-war governments.

A dedicated researcher, an experienced and able administrator, Mary Hanbidge conducted her campaign without evident recourse to the universities in Dublin where, in the 1930s, the study of Irish history was being professionalised. Instead, she found state agencies such as the National Library and what she terms 'the Public Record Office of Ireland (Oifig Iris Puibli)' more accessible. Local history was (indeed, is) a passionate liturgy of what is nowadays called Irishness, often involving a subjective enthusiasm and presumptive nationalism both of which were suspect in the eyes of professors T. W. Moody (Trinity College) and Robin Dudley Edwards (University College) in Dublin. Mary Hanbidge's acknowledged advisers worked outside the forum of higher education – the Celtic scholar Richard Irvine Best (who was Librarian at the National Library), the political historian Charles Dickson, and the onomasticist (or place-name specialist) Liam Price.

Genealogy, first cousin to local history, has noble precedent in the Gaelic annals, and has acquired new energies in the twentieth century with the enthusiasm of visiting Irish Americans in search of their 'roots'. Here, too, the universities had little to offer Mary Hanbidge, whose concern was neither a classic case of emigration and worldly success nor of victimisation and devotion to Holy Ireland. Given her own absorption into the British educational system, and the absence in her inheritance of those formative experiences which produced the Irish Free State, one might have expected her to relate positively towards Northern Ireland. Neither her research as published here, nor the commentary of younger family members, suggest anything of the kind. Her Irish concerns were exclusively local, yet they in no way inhibited her acceptance of the new situation in Dublin. She does not, however, seem to have given much thought to any notion of retirement back to Wicklow.

With the completion of work by the binders (probably early in 1940), Mary Hanbidge had two loose sheets of paper printed. One of these carried 'Appendix C' to her father's *Memories* though the contents page made no reference to such a thing, clearly an after-thought or *samizdat*. The appendix begins with some remarks about his brother Joseph and his laziness which had been retained in the main text as published, but continues with more delicate revelations. Brother John, admittedly under provocation by his wife, had 'turned libertine following other women'. These note-like obser-vations conclude with the reference to Mrs Valentine's murder in 1798 already referred to. From them one gains a reinforced sense of William Hanbidge's willingness to tell his tale ungarnished and undisguised, together with an apprehension of his daughter's concern for the feelings of others whose kith and kin were so plainly depicted.

At the outset, the editor had declared in her Foreword, 'It is printed exactly as he wrote it; spelling, punctuation and capitals, paragraphs and divisions are his: nothing is altered, but there are one or two omissions of matters which he wrote for his children only, with no thought of publication.' Perhaps these are fully pre-served in the folded single sheet carrying Appendix C; perhaps there are other details yet to be traced. Unfortunately, Mary Hanbidge's original typescript or manuscript has not been located. The impact of the war, her own unmarried and isolated situation, and the non-commercial nature of the publication contributed to this loss. It is ironic that the successor volume to the *Memories*, edited with great care by Nora Hanbidge of Barraderry, was unable to provide a date for the death of Mary Hanbidge, the chronicler unchronicled.

The second sheet of paper printed up at the time of binding the *Memories* – or perhaps later – was essentially what the trade calls a 'flyer'. The book's contents are described, accompanied by a recommendation by Richard Best. The existence of this item suggests that there had been an intention to sell copies of the book or perhaps to seek reviews in magazines and newspapers. All the surviving evidence indicates that little of the kind occurred. Wartime restrictions on travel between Britain and Ireland, the imposition of economies in the use of paper in Britain, led to its neglect. Numerous members of the Hanbidge family were given their personal copy by the editor, and there distribution effectively ended.

One could seek parallels to the unusual story of the *Memories*, its composition and release, but the results will do little to mitigate the uniqueness of the Hanbidges' experience. At the local level, there is the story of Alice Wheatley, born and brought up near Avoca in East Wicklow in a house very similar to Tinnahinch. Leaving behind several farming brothers who remained unmarried, she pursued an education, became a nurse, and eventually was appointed Matron of the Route Hospital in County Antrim. But the Wheatley story involves a migration from independent Ireland to Northern Ireland which no Hanbidge appears to have contemplated. At the literary level, there is the novel *The Heat of the Day* (1949) by Elizabeth Bowen, a highly complex account of wartime loyalties divided between Ireland and England, occurring not at the level of small-farmer Protestantism but in the milieu of the Big House.

After the War, Mary Hanbidge settled in Torquay, on the English south coast. Another scion of Irish Protestantism lived in the area, though there is no evidence that she ever met Sean O'Casey (1880–1964). She died on 13 August 1951 at the age of 85. A committee was appointed in the Central Foundation Girls' School to decide upon an appropriate commemoration. As the former head-mistress had greatly admired an early nineteenth-century statue depicting two pupils of the precursor institution, a replica was commissioned from a Polish sculptor named Ossowsky, whose

'Gog and Magog' stood outside London's Guildhall. His work now serves as her memorial in the re-sited Foundation School.

III A PERSONAL NOTE

I should move to conclude with a personal admission. My father was born on 30 July 1897 in a tenement house in York Street, Dublin, the ground-landlords being members of the Synge family. His mother, Sarah (1864–1918), is said to have been the daughter of Henry Hanbidge and his wife Ellen Giltrap; certainly she married my grandfather Charles Tresham Mac Cormack on 2 February 1887. The local, but hardly close, association of Hanbidges and Synges (turned Synge-Hutchinson) in West Wicklow lends some credence to rival explanations of my father's birth on a Synge floor now proposed. Both are consistent with family trees devised by Mary Hanbidge, but are not explicitly confirmed by them – viz (1) my great-grandfather may have been a Henry Hanbidge who emigrated to Toronto (according to Mary Hanbidge's genealogy) or (2) may have been a brother of our author (Mr Ken Hanbidge's suggestion). In practice, it has not proved desirable to transplant the groves of genealogy nurtured by Miss Hanbidge, nor would they resolve the issue of my Hanbidge great-grandfather's identity.

It is of course shocking to be so unsure of these lineal authentifications, for one can hardly hold one's head up in decent society without a pedigree for support. There is, however, a strange and even sinister double connection, again local if not close. George Plant's sister married into an East Wicklow family, into which one of my mother's kin also married. When Plant was confined in Arbour Hill during the long and bizarre preliminaries which led to his execution in Portlaoise, it was to this sister in East Wicklow than he directed his permitted quota of letters, communications of psychotic cheerfulness. Perhaps a moral for researchers is discernible: if you can claim kinship with genial and kindly Billy Hanbidge, you have to accept kinship with genial and killing George Plant. Indeed, an analysis of the Hanbidge *Memories* had already begun to disclose this shadow of its Christian virtue through the lacunae conveniently named Holt and Parnell, disruptive forces arising out of the rough materials we have for identity, the one scarcely literate, the other obstructively eloquent, paradoxes of the Word.

There remains one uncomfortable final point to be made about William Hanbidge, uncomfortable but at least impersonal. It concerns both his religious views and his relations with James Joyce, an unexpected convergence. Hanbidge was born into the Established Church, baptised and married in it. Nevertheless, he worked closely with nonconformists in London and, while in New York, could admire the devotion of Catholic priests to their flock. In practical terms, he was an ecumenist before his time. A number of his stories suggest that clerical ordination did not appeal, not simply because he lacked formal education but because he regarded the role of clergymen as decidedly secondary to the personal relationship the soul could have with God. This is decidedly *low* in ecclesiological and theological terms. Yet there is little to suggest the Calvinist in Hanbidge, no 'terrible doctrine' (Calvin's own term) of reprobation. Here, paradoxically, he takes his place close to Usher's Island in Joyce's ultimate story of Dublin, 'The Dead'. Like the Morkans and the more thoughtful among their guests, Hanbidge is a *survivor* of the nineteenth century. His brand of Christianity served this end as it served other, higher ends. Not for him a retrospective 'Faith of Our Fathers' Holy God / In Spite of Dungeon, Fire and Sword', but a faith transmissible to his daughter in the Central Foundation Girls' School, Spital Square.

Parnell the constitutionalist had private thoughts about fire and sword. He was fascinated by recollections of the rebellion in

Wicklow, especially by tales of cruel punishment and stoic endurance of pain. Yeats in turn was fascinated by Parnell, especially by a
story or fantasy of the Chief's tearing the flesh of his own palms in
an effort at self-control under provocation. (Here, the Chief of
Yeats becomes a kind of Do-It-Yourself Christ, crucifying his
own hands with his own nails.) These violent emblemisations of
'Protestant Ascendancy' in crisis have no time for the Hanbidges
and Plants of 1810. If William omits The Chief, the Chief's self-
appointed laureate omits all below the plimsoll line, including even
those Dunlavin Mollinixes fallen from the social standing of
William Molyneux whose *Case of Ireland's Being Bound by Acts of
Parliament in England* (1698) is taken as a founding document of
colonial nationalism. From this underworld of Protestant descen-
dancy, few voices have been heard, their audibility dictated along
lines of nationalist convergence. William Hanbidge is a remarkable
exception, even if it has taken a century for his words to reach a
wider audience than the kith and kin he loved.

I was most recently in the Glen of Imaal on Sunday 5 September
2004. A few Scots pine stood with all their battered vigilance on the
horizon. The light was near perfect, the still air likewise, water lay
briefly in the river. Single-storey Tinnahinch lay behind me, its
fondly preserved corrugated roof out of sight. I chose to switch on
the car radio for a news bulletin: the cumulative, horrifying tally
from Beslan had jumped to 322, mainly children. A diary told me
that the day was the festival of Saint Bartholomew, on which day in
1572 the king of France massacred thousands of Huguenot
Protestants in Paris and in provincial towns. Dunlavin seemed
remote. Later on a Hanbidge television, I watched the Russian
mothers, heard their dropped flowers flopping on the road to the
cemetery. We need the likes of *Memories of West Wicklow* to save us
from despair.

A Note on the Texts

Mary Ann Hanbidge published *The Memories of William Hanbidge Aged 93. 1906: An Autobiography* in very late 1939 or early 1940. In fact, the book was printed in St Albans for private circulation, and it is not clear how many copies were issued or how many can now be traced. It is certainly a scarce item.

William Hanbidge's writings occupy only pp. 19–57 of more than 300 pp., though his daughter's extensive notes and appendices contain scattered sentences and remarks of which he was the author. The present edition aims to include all that was his, together with such of the daughter's further annotations and appendices as are useful to general readers. Her contribution is to be found in two distinct modes – (1) annotations to her father's text which are preserved here as such, though edited for economy on a few occasions; (2) longer essay-like pieces now displayed for the first time in their own integrity.

There remains a good deal of Miss Hanbidge's publication which is not reproduced here – this includes original research on the origins of the family in Gloucester and Hereford, the diaspora of various branches to Canada and New Zealand, sundry family trees somewhat awkwardly presented, a great deal of superfluous comment (for example on the Poor Law), and a touching if repetitious tribute to family sentiment.

The 1939 edition was assembled in retirement, more than thirty years after William Hanbidge's death. The work was accomplished partly through research in Britain, partly through correspondence with relatives round the world, and – most importantly – through visits to Dublin, Dundalk and Wicklow. The death of the editor's brother in 1936 gave poignancy to the enterprise, and the deteriorating state of European affairs cast a shadow over completion of the book. The final pages are deeply scored with *pietas*, domestic and national, and it may be inferred that a thorough revision was abandoned in favour of publication before warfare prevented. Nevertheless, the resulting volume was handsomely produced, with many photographs. Most important among these are reproductions of pages from William Hanbidge's holograph.

Miss Hanbidge took the task of editing her father's writing very seriously. Her determination to remain faithful to his script, even in all its accidentals, is to be admired. It may be an unsought tribute to T. W. Moody's obsessively exact rules for contributors to *Irish Historical Studies*, or to the guidelines for contributors to Section C of the *Proceedings of the Royal Irish Academy*. One way or another, Mary Hanbidge was clearly in touch with professional historians in the course of her labours.

One intriguing aspect of William Hanbidge's handwriting style (in so far as we can gauge it from a few pages in photo reproduction of the holograph, and from his daughter's careful editing) concerns his use of the full stop or period. Generally, but not invariably, he concludes a sentence conventionally with this punctuation mark, while omitting to do so when the sentence concludes a paragraph.

The present edition has attempted a compromise between fidelity and standardisation. Hanbidge's exceedingly brief paragraphs have often been run into each other, so as to enhance the appearance and readability of the text. His fitful punctuation has been augmented with commas etc., whenever the doing so reduces ambiguity or confusion. His spelling, however, has generally been retained.

I am grateful to Ciaran Brady of Tinahely, Thomas and Nora Hanbidge of Barraderry, and Ken Hanbidge of Donard for their advice on several matters of interpretation. Also to Alan and Rosemary Hanbidge of Brockna for their hospitality. Barbara Mennell has once again proved herself an editor of exceptional patience and sensitivity.

W. J. Mc C.

William Hanbidge's Memories

✦

A few thoughts of my young days

From the register of the Church of Donoughmore County Wicklow Ireland I read that I was baptized on the seventh of June 1813: and from information derived from my brother Henry, (6 years older than me) my birthday must have been about the middle of April, so I have counted the 16th of that month as my natal day. My recollections of the first four years of my life are entirely void only that I remember sitting in the servant girl's lap facing the kitchen door while an old man named Ned Flynn

The first page of *Memories*

A Few Thoughts of My Young Days

From the register of the Church of Donoughmore County
Wicklow Ireland I read that I was baptized on the seventh of June
1813: and from information derived from my brother Henry (six
years older than me), my birthday must have been about the middle
of April,[1] so I have counted the 16th of that month as my natal day.
My recollections of the first four years of my life are entirely void
only that I remember sitting in the servant girl's lap facing the
kitchen door while an old man named Ned Flynn was inoculating
me. The next incident I remember is that one day I found a key, and
as was a believer of a doctrine prevalent in those days, that finders
should be keepers, I refused to give up the key to my mother and
got thrashed,[2] so I started off to the brook to tell my grievance to
dear Biddy Carpenter (who loved me above all people (as I did
her)),[3] and on my way was met by an old cow called Spotty which
tossed me up with her horns into the air when my head was cut. I
was carried in and remember that my grandmother was dressing
my cut head and calling me a bad boy.

I think that must have been in 1818 which was the wettest year
that has been in Ireland since: which ruined nearly all the crops.[4] I
have a much more vivid recollection of things which happened in
the year 1819 for one morning my brothers Bob and Ned were

sorting potatoes in an outhouse when they said to one another that the potatoes were small,[5] when I said if we had them last year we would have been glad of them.

As far as I can remember the summer of 1819 was the happiest of my young life. The reason was the cattle had to be kept from breaking into the crops on one side of the pasture, and from crossing the river Slaney on the other side. My dear brother Robert (four years older than myself) was to mind them so I spent my time with him. We amused ourselves in various ways. One of which was, we got some small stones ½ to 1 lb in weight off of the river strand and carried them to a big stone and called them cows,[6] and arranged them along the stone's side and got moss for hay and used to pretend to turn them out and bring them in as we did the cows only much oftener.

What I used to do in the evenings of those days or during the winter months I entirely forget.

One incident which did not happen every day occurred. A lad from one of our near neighbours named Harry Merrin was going back to his employers (Jones of the bog) with a pair of sheep shears which father had borrowed came where we were and challenged us to fight him. The fight began and Merrin poured such a shower of blows on me that I cried out to my brother to relieve me. So Bob pushed me back and whispered to me to take charge of the shears, and faced Merrin alone when the fight ended by Bob smiting Merrin on the nose and drawing a stream of blood when he began to cry and threaten what not he would do to any of our family whenever or wherever he met any of them.

'Yes', said my brother, 'you might beat the child here but as for me I am well able to lick you at any time I may meet you'.

Many years after when I used to get into the field opposite Donoughmore school where he was mowing Mr Peter Plant's meadows he and I had many a hearty laugh over our fight of our younger days.

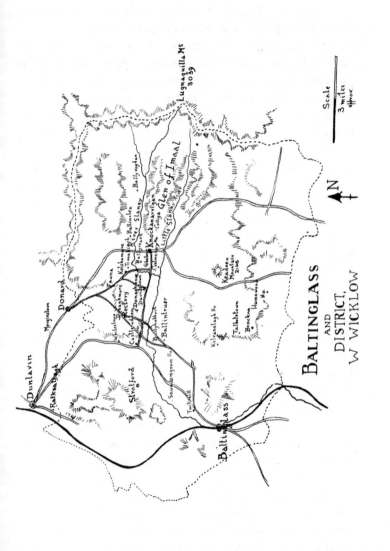

BALTINGLASS
AND
DISTRICT,
W WICKLOW

Scale
3 miles
approx.

N

Lugnaquilla Mt
3039

Little Slaney River

Glen of Imaal

River Slaney

Ballyvogan

Knocknarrigan

Ballinclea

Kadeen Mountain 2152

Ballinabrany

Coline

Donard

Merginstown

Rathcoran

Dunlavin

Stratford

Saundersgrove Ho

Rampere

Tuckmill

Baltinglass

Kilranelagh Ho

Talbotstown

Brockna

Humewood Ho

Ballitore

Belan

Donoughmore

Rectory

Castleruddery

Whitestown

Ballynure

I suppose why I do not remember anything about the evenings of 1819 is that I used to fall asleep and go to bed.

In the beginning of the summer of 1820 I went into the room where father and mother were at breakfast when father said 'Billy boy which will you go to school or mind the cows?' I promptly said 'Mind, mind the cows', but of that more hereafter.

I must now introduce two new personages into my history. One an old woman named Katty Burns who went by the name of Katty the Shed, because she lived in a most miserable hut on the side of Kaudeen Mountain, and Dick Lewis of Donard whose usual title was Bachelor Lewis. In those days there were no poorhouses[7] so that there were many people who went about the country from door to door begging of whom Katty Burns was one and a favoured one at my old home, who used to say to me if she ever met me out she would carry me off.

My dear mother one day sent me to Knockinargen[8] to a shop where she got her groceries for the first time with full instructions that I should not go astray (which I was nearly doing) and on my way home who should I meet on Gibstown Cross roads but Katty. 'Oh now I have you', she said, and I with tears in my eyes stretched out my hand towards her and she seeing my distress let me go. After that I was always a favourite with her. When I left home for good and come back at Easter for my annual holiday she was sure to come to see me.

Dick Lewis was a butcher who lived in the little town of Donard. He was quite a terror to all the children who met him, often came to my father's on business and threatened to eat me if he ever met me. One day I was coming down Kelsha Hill and to my horror of horrors who should I meet but Lewis who when he saw me began to dance and cut capers. I made a few attempts to get past him but failed so being rendered desperate I took up two or three stones and threatened to knock his brains out if he did not let me pass which after another caper he did. I met him a few years after at father's and he told my father that he never got such a fright in his life when he saw me get the stones. I assured him that he had very good reason.

Another incident I must not pass over. One day me and some of my brothers were playing in what we called the Bottoms under the big bank.[9] Our play was jumping up and down a ditch over what was called a gripe full of black mud. I jumped down very well but when I made an attempt to jump up I fell into the black mud and was pulled out of the gripe as black as a mudlark. I went home roaring as loud as the braying of a jack ass. Unfortunately for me I fell into the hands of my father who gave me such a whipping with his hard hand that I should not have forgotten it in a hurry. My mother and that old friend of mine cleaned my clothes and when I was dressed I started off again. This time I determined to keep clear of the gripe and to run another way so I jumped over a drain but there was another within a couple of yards of it into which I tumbled and when I got out I was again covered with black mud. Home I went again but this time with much less noise than on my former mishap when mother and Biddy stripped me and put me to bed and as I soon fell asleep the poor child did not get into any more trouble that day.

Up to that time I do not remember ever to have seen Donoughmore church or Davidstown chapel[10] or my grandfather's, or my uncles, so that the first 6 years of my life were spent in a very circumsiced [*sic*] space.

Before proceeding farther I will here give an account of my dear mother's industry, of course assisted by my father.

My father used to sow some flax-seed every spring which when grown up and in blossom was a beautiful sight to see such a beautiful blue blossom. This flax in due time was pulled up and tied in sheaves and carted off to the blind arch of Kelsha Bride[11] and put under water (bogged as they called it) to help to separate the fibre from the stalk. After a few weeks' time it was taken up and carted back and spread on the new mown meadow to dry. When it was dry it was tied up into large (now) white bundles and put up in a safe place till winter when it was dried on a hurdle over a fire broke with a brake, skutched carded or hackled.[12] Then the flax was spun by my mother and sister Betty and it was music indeed to all who sat around the fire to hear the spinning wheels. A pound weight of flax was spun into hanks of yarn each twelve cuts containing 120 threads which were sent to Jack Flynn[13] who wove it into linen for which he charged 6*d.* per yard. Out of the tow of the flax they spun yarn of which they made table, cloths, linsey, sheets &c. and of the very coarsest big sacks which could hold 40 stone of potatoes. Mother and sister spun it all.

Nearly every thing we wore my mother got manufactured. Of wool our coats our flannels our stockings the linsey woolsey for their own wear. Old nanny Myers was engaged to spin the wool for the freize [*sic*] every year.[14] When the yarn was ready it was sent to Jack Flynn to be woven and when woven then to the dyers in Donard who before dying sent it to the tuckmill. It came home a beautiful light drab which was easily soiled.

Nearly all the Irish counties had different coloured friezes so that each man wherever he went was known by the colour of his coat.[15] All the rest of the wool for blankets flannels stockings &c was spun by mother. For several days after the freize [*sic*] was brought home Joe Gougher the tailor had a busy time of it, as there were father and five sons.

So much for my dear mother's industry.

My father's lay in a different manner for besides farming he used to buy pigs to kill and make bacon of to send to the Dublin market[16] sometimes he lost money and more times he gained but on the whole if he had the fall of the pigs for his labour he was satisfied. Irish bacon used to waste greatly in cooking as the pigs while fattening got nothing better than potatoes but in after years when those who fed them fed them with corn the bacon found its way to London where it was bought in such quantities as almost to oust English bacon out of the London market. The Irish in its turn was ousted out of the poorer parts of London by Canadian.

About our living in my younger days we got potatoes and milk for breakfast. Our milk in wooden noggins, and the things used for plates were wooden trenchers which in time were superseded by tin pannicans and very bad white delft white plates[17] which improved in their looks by green and blue edges, afterwards by the blue willow pattern traces of which are to be found in the houses till this day one thousand nine hundred and six. Mother used to come with her dish to get a few flowery [sic] potatoes to mix them with flour to make a cake for father and her breakfast bake it on a hot griddle or pan and when sufficiently baked serve it up well buttered which when I used to get a piece of I found it much more palatable than the potatoes and milk.

Our dinners varied sometimes pigs meat, eggs and butter but very often the same as we had for breakfast.[18]

We had no egg cups or egg spoons so we propped them up with potatoes and eat them with the end of the iron spoons with which we used to eat our stirabout in spring as there were not a small spoon in the house safe six silver ones which father bought when he got married.

Our suppers were the same as our breakfasts.

Very few equalled my mother as a butter maker.[19] Her butter always got the top price in the Dublin butter market.

I will here write a short account of Stratford on Slaney, its people and their employment. It was about three miles from my old home built on the side of a hill so that it stood on high ground in the midst of an agricultural district. It was more noted for a cotton manufactory carried on by a Mr Orr who employed large numbers of cotton weavers with their fly shuttles, also bleachers, cutters and printers.

A Mr Burnside designed all the patterns. A Mr Glynn engraved them and young men of the town were taught to cut the blocks which the printers used in stamping the calico. But after it being woven it was bleached before it was sent to the printers. Mr Orr shipped the greatest part to South America. Stratford was a very busy place. There were two markets held in it weekly[,] one on Wednesday, the other on Saturday to which the surrounding farmers sent potatoes. The butchers of Donard brought meat, but a drawback on the trade was that the buyers used to pay in Mr Orr's I.O.U's which readily passed in Baltinglass. Stratford was a prosperous little place but it was also a most abominable wicked place. The scenes to be seen of a Saturday nights and on Sundays were awful. Drunkenness, prostitution, cursing and fighting.

There were always a wordy warfare carried on between the country and town lads for the country lads when they saw the weavers would shout 'A dish of kailcannon and an iron spoon'[20] would make any calico weaver jump over his loom with other scurrilous epithets which the others resented very much. All used to meet at a low public house about half a mile from the town on Saturday evenings and Sundays the sights which followed I cannot describe.

After a time the downfall of the town began. Mr Orr found out that he could buy the calico ready wo[ven] much cheaper than it cost him to have it woven so he dismissed all his weavers who were scattered over many parts of England and Scotland. The slated houses which they lived in soon fell into ruin.[21] Mr Orr still continued the bleaching and printing business for a short time till his correspondent in South America failed by which he lost thousands of pounds and he turned bankrupt and could not continue the business. All the remaining employees had to seek work in England or Scotland and others such as shoemakers &c.

Thus fell Stratford – no more markets.

MY SCHOOL DAYS

When I found that I had to mind the cows by myself I changed my mind and went to school[22] to Mr Ivers who had a sort of hedge school on Mr Peter Valentine's land.[23] There were many grown up young men attending, with some of them I was a great favourite during play time. I used to go amongst them with book in hand to be taught my letters.

I remember well to go to a William Hawkins to be taught when he pointed to a big M and I repeated the letters to myself (as I had them off by rote) then said 'M'. 'You are a rogue', he said. I do not think I was very long in learning them and little words for the next thing I remember was learning words of two syllables with a girl. The columns we divided in three parts three of which we learned in the morning and two in the afternoon and skipped the third part for we always commenced a fresh line next day.

When I used to go up to Mr Ivers to hear me my lessons if he did not at once take heed to me I used to put my hand into his bosom.

At play time during the dinner hour some of us young ones used to race but Charley Ivers (the master's son) was always able to run me down. The school was closed in winter. At that time I never heard of Lancaster or his system of education although it was in force in a few schools, for a philanthropic gentleman named Erasmus Smith[24] had endowed schools in many parts of Ireland on the conditions that if any gentleman would give a house and two acres of land rent free he would give thirty pounds yearly. One drawback to his scheme was the appointing of incompetent and untrained teachers to the schools. The teachers only could teach reading, writing and arithmetic (with the help of a key). They knew nothing of English grammar or geography. As for trained teachers there were scarcely any for there were no training schools save Kildare Street, [25] where Lancaster's system was taught but little else save in the female department where they taught the teachers needlework and embroidery.

That we might not forget what we learned in summer my father engaged a man named Kit Coulter to come some days in the week to teach me and my brothers when I learned more spelling but I forget if I were as yet taught to read. [26]

As regards religious instruction I never had any up to this time only that I think either now or next year my dear mother taught me the church Catechism. During the winter months of 1820–21, Mr Greene[27] the curate of Donoughmore used to come to Mrs Plant's house (who was sextoness of the Church).[28] Once a week we all stood in her kitchen the big ones behind and such as I was in the front and when I would strive to hide amongst the big boys he would bring me forward. I do not remember a word of his teaching.

It was in the spring of 1821 I began to go to church when on Sunday mornings we sat around and inside the communion rails for instruction in scriptural knowledge but when the parish school was opened in June we all migrated thither. My teacher was Miss Greene, Mr Greene's eldest sister.

I attended the opening of the school the first day (a very little fellow when compared to some of the big ones) and continued (not very regularly as I was kept too often at home first to mind the cows afterwards as I grew in stature and strength to help in spring haymaking, reaping and potatoe [*sic*] digging) till the autumn of 1829, when I left to go to a training school in Dublin.

When I first entered the school I soon learned to read write arithmetic and scripture. We used to write on slates with pencils of the same material. My first attempt at writing was with my left hand[29] but as I had to use my right hand I felt very awkward but I soon got over that but I could on slates write almost as well with my left hand as with my right. I could make capital letters quite as well. I got through nearly all Thompson's Arithmetic which gave a reason for every rule throughout his book.[30]

Our chief teaching was scripture[31] for Mr Greene came twice a week to the school and expounded the meaning of a chapter or two which we had previously been instructed in by a girl named Eliza Styles whom the schoolmaster got as an app[r]entice out of the Foundling hospital James St. Dublin.[32]

At last as I have before stated I was sent to the Training school[33] which was held in a house on the premises of the Foundling hospital where we never were allowed out into the streets unless on Sundays [*sic*] afternoons and not then if we had not given satisfaction in our studies the previous week. The Head of the school was a Mr James Aiken[34] and his Usher a Mr James Walsh. I made fair progress in Geography, Grammar, Scripture learned some of Euclid. I wrote out the whole of Bell's system of education and the whole of Walker's philosophy of Arithmetic and was well instructed in Pestalozzo's mental Arithmetic, Arithmetic which greatly expanded the mind.

I must now go back to my sunday [*sic*] school days for as I have before written we migrated from the Communion rails of the church to the new School. Mr Greene was at the school every Sunday morning punctual at 10.30 and taught a class of the more grown ones till nearly 12 o'c[lock] while the young ones were taught by others. I was still in Miss Greene's class and she used to shew me her pinch back watch and taught me to know the time. Did I not but think that the watch was a grand sight. We got by heart (as we expressed) the collect for the day.

We went up to church at 12 o'c and when the service was over we came back to school again for more instruction. The younger ones were dismissed about 3 o'c but Mr Greene kept the elder ones for another hour and when I had grown up to be counted an elder one I never got home in winter to eat my dinner till it was dark.

There was a lending library.[35] Also we all got a piece of white bread (if we had had our scripture lessons) which I assure you I enjoyed very much. I have been several times in the morning sunday school since Mr Greene's severance from the parish but it was Ichabod, Ichabod the glory had departed.[36] The afternoon one had been discontinued.

Mr Greene lived at his father's in Kilranalagh which was I may say surrounded by a portion of three parishes Kilranalagh, Donoughmore and Baltinglass and near to the house (but in Donoughmore parish) was one of the Erasmus Smith's schools of which his father was patron. Every Saturday at this school very many of the protestant boys and girls of the three parishes used to attend. Mr Greene used to have the elder ones in a class in the school while all the younger ones went over to the big house and were instructed by his father, stepmother and three sisters. I found my way to this school although I lived fully four Irish miles from it.[37]

There used to be examinations every Christmas time under the auspices of the Association for Discountenancing Vice who gave prizes to those who answered best. In 1824 I felt disgraced for though I had well prepared for the examination by reading the portions of scripture we were to be examined in I scarcely answered a question[38] but I made up for defeat by winning the prizes[39] the two following years, 1825, [182]6.

After my return from the Training school I staid at home from November 1830 till June 1832 when I was appointed master of my old school where I remained till February 1837[40] when I went to Dublin to be a clerk to a solicitor and my wife[41] to keep a shop, but as I did not succeed in business I had to go back to school teaching. I got an appointment in the Parish of Clonmore County Carlow under Archdeacon Stopford a son of the Earl of Courtown County Wexford. [42] I met a cousin of my father's in that parish and made many kind friends still I could not stop as my wife's health began to fail through the effects of a very damp house so I removed to Athy County Kildare the beginning of 1840 where my wife's health got worse and worse. Every day she had to give up teaching and having had another baby she went home to her father's where she died on the 20th of January 1841, leaving a sickly baby and four other children the eldest of whom was only seven years old the day her dear mother was buried.

After my wife's death I got a school in the Parish of Carbury County Kildare and in that school[43] and in Killina I remained eleven years when I went to Kilranalagh where I staid nearly six years then I came to London and worked in the City Mission 36 years and was pensioned off January 1st 1894 and here I am now a very old man nearly 93 years of age.

As my story has become an autibiography [*sic*] I now give some more incidents of my life and of my brothers and sisters. My father and mother were the parents of nine sons and two daughters viz Elizabeth born in 1795, John born in 1798 (the year of the Irish rebellion), Joseph born in 1801, William, Tom[44] and a premature birth born between the years 1801 and 1807, Henry born in 1807, Robert (called Bob) born in 1809, Edward (called Ned), myself

William (called Billy) and Catharine (called Kitty). Ned was born in 1811, self born in 1813, Kitty born in 1815 about three months after the battle of Waterloo.

I was a very mischiefous [*sic*] fellow and not over scrupulous as to lying and pilfering. Aye even one day I turned highway robber for there was a poor woman's son who attended the school where I also attended who wore an old livery coat with large livery buttons on it one of which I coveted, so one day when I met him I cut it off in pretending to look at it and threatened to thrash him when he complained he never told the school master.[45]

My sister Kitty grew up and married a man in Dunlavin named John Thomas who shortly after burst a blood vessel and ever after was very infirm. They had a large family the majority of them died of consumption as did their father in December 1858 and their mother in July 1860.[46]

I should have said I was in danger of being killed twice, once by a carpenter named Barney Flynn who threw a hatchet at me and split the side of my nose, second by falling off of a creef of turf on the top of which John Jones (a first cousin of my father's) was given me a ride one of my school fellows sitting on the back of the car tilting it as there was no belly band to the car.

My brother Ned was always a hard work[er] and used to get up every morning in summer and autumn very early to look after the cattle. He got the old place and married Anne Douglas a daughter of Mr William Douglas of Kyle. They had a large family of daughters viz Lizzie, Sarah, Anne, Kitty (called Kate), Jane, Mary and Martha also three sons John, William and Edward. John died when he was about seven years of age (which almost broke his mother's heart), Willie and Eddie the very best boys in the parish. Sarah and Mary when they were grown up to womanhood. Some babies died in infancy.

My brother got rich through the work of his sons. A few years before my brother's death he bought a small farm which was very near the old home. Four of the girls got married all of whom now are widows. Martha and the two boys are still single. My brother's wife died when a little over 70 years of age and he followed a few years afterwards on the 26th January 1899, leaving the farms to his son William.[47] He was within a few weeks of 87 years of age. Buried in Donoughmore.

My brother Robert was much given to fishing in the river Slaney with a rod.[48] So on wet days when we could not stay out in the fields when we came indoors instead of drying his clothes as the rest of us did, used to be tying flies for fishing, so laid the foundation of an early death.

He married Eliza Crampton and had two sons Robert and John. He lived on his brother John's farm (more about it hereafter). He died rather unexpectedly in the April of 1853 aged 44 years and was buried in Donoughmore.

Brother Henry was one of the best sons a father ever had. One of the best workers. He lived at the old Home full 40 years. He was on the whole kind to the young ones of us that is Kitty and I. He got a farm in Kiltegan Parish but there were no dwelling or out houses on it till he built a small dwelling house (afterwards turned into a stable when he had built a large dwelling house), barn cow house &c. Now it is like a small village. He married Martha Douglas a younger sister of his brother Edward's wife. They had ten children viz John now living in Liverpool, William now owner of the farm, Sarah now living in Dublin, Henry, Elizabeth, Edward, Samuel, Tom, Martha and a baby that did not live many days.

Henry spent 28 years in the Royal Constabulary, got to the top of the tree amongst the uncommissioned officers and then retired on a good pension of 64 pounds sterling yearly.[49] Then was appointed to be an inspector by the society for preventing cruelty to women and children. Now he is in the town Lancaster married and has a wife and two little girls.

Elizabeth lives with a husband in Co. Westmeath, Ireland. Edward is now land steward for Lord Mayo near Naas County Kildare, Ireland Samuel on the farm helping his brother to farm and to buy and sell cattle. Tom joined the Royal Irish Constabulary and is now in Tullamore (Serjeant). He married some years ago but his wife soon died leaving one son who has been brought up by his grandmother Hanbidge and will very probably be heir of all as their is no likelihood of his uncles William or Sam marrying.

Martha helps her mother in house work. I may call her a poultry farmer. It often amused me to [watch/see] a couple of hundred of hens chickens following her across the yard to be fed.[50]

My dear brother did no work for years but only went about the farm with a thistle stubber in his hand (instead of a stick) and wherever he saw a thistle he stubbed it up. He was a big fat man one time 18 stone weight but wasted in flesh greatly till at last he died the last days of the year 1894 full of days as he only wanted a few weeks of being 87 years and was buried in Kiltegan Churchyard. He and I loved one another dearly. At the head of his own table he looked like a patriarch. He was very hospitable and greatly respected both by his poor and rich neighbours. He fed some of the best veal calves that ever were seen in the market in Dublin.

My brother Joe was I believe born lazy; at least he showed that he was very early in his life[.] So father used to say I will give you a trade consequently he was sent to his Uncle Bob in Stratford to learn shoemaking. He married a nice young woman named Margaret Finlay and then went to live with her at her mother's but was always in want. He had three daughters Eliza, Margaret and Kitty and a boy who died in babyhood. He often came home especially on Sundays but things always went ill with him. He always loved me. As shoemaking failed with him he got into the Irish

Constabulary and was stationed in the County Kildare near Dublin but there things did not seem to go well with him. He left Kildare and joined the Dublin Police [51] where they had to do police duty punctually night and day which caused his health to fail so he had to resign and come back to his native parish where he lived a short time in a cottage in Whitestown thence to Kiltegan, Hacketstown. He was buried with his first wife in the church yard of that parish.

Next comes my eldest brother John was a diligent man at work. He was unable to keep his farm so he gave up the farm to his brother Robert. He died in 1882 at the age of 84 yrs and his brother Henry buried him in Donoughmore Church yard.

My dear sister Betty did not marry. She died in 1839 aged 44 years and was buried in Donoughmore C[hurch] yard. My dear mother continued an active old lady till November 1855 when she was attacked with consumption of the bowels which caused her to gallop to death in four months aged 84 and was buried in Donoughmore Church yard.

My dear father at the time of my mother's death had been confined to his bed nearly two years and was almost unconscious of her death. He outlived her [by] two years eight months, bedridden all the time [and] died the 28th November 1858 (one day short of 90 ? years).[52] He was buried alongside of dear mother.

I am now come to the end of all my family but I must mention dear old Biddy Carpenter[. M]y father's successor on the farm was very poor and so was I at the time[53] so she had to enter the poors house[54] of Baltinglass union where she died and was buried in a pauper's grave on the side of Baltinglass hill which had been set apart for that purpose.

SPORTS

One day I remember a meeting for wrestling took place near to the old druidical remains in part of Kelshamore when my brother John overthrew Ned Nolan of Davidstown who was one of the finest young men in the parish and Nid Jones (a first cousin of my father's) overthrew a man named Kenny who was nearly twice his size. I used to wrestle a lad name Pennefather who lived at father's who used to over throw me but like a tribe of old I over came at the last.

I now let my thoughts go back to my training school days to add a few more words about it. Our Principal the Revd James Aikin when he was entering into the school room of mornings used to make such a noise as almost to frighten my life out at least it set me trembling but I understood the meaning afterwards that it was kindness.

I have said that Mr Greene curate of Donoughmore Parish who suggested and recommended me for the Training school. He came to see me one day when it happened to be the day that Doctor Murray (the Chaplain of the Foundling Hospital) came into the school to hear read the report of our diligence at our studies. There were seven week reports and I was the only one who had very good for the whole seven.

Mr Greene Mr Greene, said the Doctor you ought to be quite proud of your boy. So he was for his eyes sparkled with joy.

At Easter I got a few holidays to go home and on Good Friday when there was a good dinner of corn beef on the table I did not wait for it as I was so anxious to get off. I made my way up to Garden Lane Francis Street where my people used to put up at one Andrew Donohoe's and met Jim Brien who lived near Donoughmore Church. (He was my mother's first cousin) so after a little talk he consented to take me home where we arrived about midnight a most glorious moonlight night.

As I would not consent to stay in Brien's house till morning I started for home and when I arrived in the yard I saw that the kitchen door had been changed.[55] I knocked at the window of the room where I used to sleep when brother Ned said who is there I answered Billy, and in a couple of seconds I was in his arms almost hugged to death. I do not remember anything about any one in the house that night only that mother was in bed and that father and Henry were out a wake of my father's uncle Edward who lived in Donard.[56] I would not go to bed but stopped up till father and Henry came home and when they knocked and I opened the door father father [*sic*] took me in his arms and almost hugged the breath out of me. I went back to the Training School the following Wednesday almost broken hearted.

I made fair progress and got punished by the Head for lending some of my manuscripts to dunces to copy. Altogether I was a pupil in the school from the 19th September 1829 till the 11th of November 1830. On leaving I got a fairly good certificate not the very best but still a very good one. We were taught no history.

I was glad to get home but that winter I went to school to learn surveying and worked on father's farm all the following year 1831 and part of 1832. During that time my grandfather died in December 1830 and my grandmother in the summer of 1832 both full of days they were buried in Dunlavin the burial place of the first Hanbidges who came to Ireland.

Another incident in the year 1831 was that I fell in love with Eliza Finlay the third daughter of Mr John Finlay of Ballineden who had with her mother come to see me while I was in the training school but as I was very young (only 18) and very shy I only saw her in Church or at the confirmation class. One day in her father's turf bog where we got our years firing both of us were spreading turf some little distance from each other when I cast many a loving look at her on my way home in the evening. I got down to a stream of water to wash off the mud where Eliza was doing the same. I made love to her which she confessed she returned so I went home one of the happiest youths in Ireland. She never knew why I gave her up. But I must say it was a bit of jealously [*sic*].[57] I never forgot her from that to this now nearly 75 years ago. Eliza went to America and was married to an old school fellow of mine. I heard that she was the mother of four sons.

In June of 1832 I commenced teaching Donoughmore school and the 15th of April 1833 I was married to Anna Rosetta Hocter to whom I had transferred my love. She was the daughter of the teacher of one of the Erasmus Smiths schools.[58] In my eyes she was a beautiful girl most lovely and had been trained in Kildare Street Training school and above [all] she was a most sincere Christian of whom I was altoger [*sic*] unworthy. Young women run great danger in marrying very young men who are too often like a child with a new doll when the paint is kissed off wants another but my mind never wandered so far as that.

My dear wife died on the 20th January 1841. At the time just three months less than 8 years after our marriage, leaving 5 children viz Anna Rosetta aged 7 years, John 5 yrs 4 month, William Hocter 3 yrs 11 months, Elizabeth 1 year 10 months, and Robert Purcell not 5 months old.

Anna Rosetta who was a simple minded was for years in delicate in [*sic*] health died in London in 1870 having caught the smallpox in visiting the poor in the vicinity of Dalston station of the North London Railway. John when he grew up joined the Irish Constabury [*sic*] but after a few years he came to London, he is still alive over 70 years of age.[59]

William came to London and went to America but he returned to England after a time went to America again and joined a whaling expedition to Artic regions[. H]e fell out with some of the officers so he left and came back to London now a trained sailor[. He] went

[on] some voyages to the far East in good seaworthy healthy ships and on his last voyage (having fallen out with the mate) he joined a coasting vessel where the bad water almost poisoned him[. T]hen being entirely upset he was sent home by one of our consuls and when [he] was landed in Southampton he made his way to London and got into St. George's Hospital where he died. His death took place on the 23rd February 1876. Buried in Abney Park Cemetry.

Elizabeth was born on the 5th March in Clonmore Parish Co Carlow. She came with me to London in 1858 and after a few years at her own request she emigrated to Tasmania where she married an Englishman named Ford who after the birth of a son left her and went to some mines in New Zealand[. S]he followed him and had to make her way on foot (carrying her baby in her arms) from Dunedin to Inch Clutha[60] where she found her husband.

In Inch Clutha there were seven more children born. Her husband died but she brought up her children respectably and in the fear and love of God. She commenced ladys nure [?= nurse] and went over the south island of New Zealand greatly respected. When she began to grow old she got an old age pension. Her three daughters mar[r]ied and were the mothers of 19 or 20 children. Four of whom have died. Now her eldest daughter's sons are beginning to think of setting up housekeeping for themselves.

Robert Purcell died about three months after his mother as he had been a sickly child from his birth. Thus ends the history of my family by Anna Rosetta Hocter.

Names and date of birth of my daughter Elizabeth's children:

William Robert born March 6th 1862
Anna Rosetta born March 26th 1864
Mary born June 17th 1866
Robert born December 20th 1868
John Hanbidge born Jany 18th 1871

Thomas Henry born May 23rd 1873
Elizabeth Jane born November 10th 1875
    All Fords

I went to teach the Church School Parish of Carbury Killina Co Kildare in the year 1844 four years previous to the great famine owing to the failure of the potatoe crop. [B]ut for some years there were many indications that the potatoe was failing for you could frequently see patches in the potatoe fields where none grew one side of a ridge looking green and healthy and the other side no sign of a potatoe stalk.[61]

I was at my old home in 1846 and as all the working hands on the farm were very busy I went out to dig potatoes for the dinner and every second potatoe was rotten. But the real cause of the famine was that the potatoes rotted in the pits and the houses although the[y] looked sound [and] good when dug out of the ground. As the scripture said of the Egyptian famine that it was sore in the land so it may well be said that it was so in Ireland in 1847. Thousands died of actual hunger, thousands and thousands of fever caused by hunger. The population of Ireland in 1841 was over eight millions and in 1851 it was but a little more than six millions.[62] All did not die but thousands fled out of the country as from a pest house.

English charity at the time sent large sums of money over to buy provisions for the hungry but then Indian Meal was three shillings per stone and oatmeal and flour and bread dear in proportion. The provinces of Leinster and Ulster did not suffer so much as Connaught and Munster[;] it was in the two latter provinces that death held carnival.

One characteristic of the Irish was that on the death of a neigbour hundreds would attend the funeral but during the famine scarcely any one went to see their neighbour.

There were subscriptions got all over the civilized world for the starving Irish and if it had not been so the poor of the two provinces would have been altogether been [*sic*] wiped out. [63]

On the 25th of March (that year of famine) I married Jane Jacob whose parents lived near to the town of Carnew Co. Wicklow. Her first and last children were still born but she also had two living ones, Jane born 23rd of September 1849 and Robert William born 19th of April 1851 but after I removed from Killina to Kilranalagh she died on the 31st of March 1853 in the same room where my first wife died. Her sister Hannah Jacob who came to my house with her sister when I was married remained till I came to London in 1858 and was as a mother to the two little ones.

The Revd Frederick Trench Rector of Cloughjordan Co Tipperary went to England and collected large sums of money from his friends and relatives and on coming back to Ireland he sent a band of gentlemen to the neighbourhood of Ballydehob Co Cork (which had suffered more than any other part of Ireland), who started soup kitchens in several parts before the Government did anything. When the Government opened soup kitchens Mr Trench withdrew his helpers and on balancing his accounts he found he had a large overplus. On consulting the subscribers they came to the conclusion that the best thing to do with the money was to send some boys who had lost their parents to America. I was chosen to go over in charge of them so I went to Cork to meet Mr Trench and his Agent Mr Allen. I preceded Mr Allen to Skibbereen and put up at a hotel and I assure you to me there was no sign of famine that night. Mr Allen came down from Cork later and next morn we started for Skull[64] and as we went along the country seemed almost a desolation. Those that we did see looked somewhat like ghosts. We stayed in Skull several days and got applications [to] take with us 25 boys the majority of whom had lost both parents.

We engaged a carman to take the boys to Cork I accompan[y]ing them Mr Allen going by coach before me. I never before witness [*sic*] so much (I cannot say dirt) filth in my life as I saw at all the places (even in Bandon) where the carman stopped at. It was not a whit better when I arrived in Cork. I stopped with the boys and one morning on turning down the bed clothes I was almost frightened to see such a swarm of vermin (bugs, lice, fleas). I immediately fled out of the house. Mr Trench had to come to Cork to see the boys and sent one back.

On the Saturday I and the boys started for Liverpool but here I must say the greatest rogues I ever met with were the women of Cork who had stalls in the streets. I do not remember how many days I had to stop in Liverpool before I got to start but while [I] was there I fell in with rogues almost a match for the Cork stall keepers.

We got to start at last in a ship called Finland which proved a very bad sailor (she was not a regular packet) but a vessel fitted up for emigrants. She had a lot of rails down in the hold which made bad worse. Most of the emigrants on board were a miserable lot of poor dirty Irish, aye much worse than dirty for some of them were over run with so that before the voyage was over all of us were not free from the pests.

One incident on board which amused me not a little was – When about the cooking place the Irish got fighting, Captain Johnson used to shout to the first mate Mr Colthurst, Mr Colthurst give those —— Irish a bucket or two of water and the avidity with which the order was obeyed was remarkable. The fighters never waited for a third bucket; two generally made peace. It afforded me some hearty laughs. On the voyage we saw a whale; when an old whaler saw he said Oh if I had that fellow in Boston would it not be a nice present for my old mother? We were constantly followed by shoals of porpo[i]ses and no steeple chasers could jump like them. Mother Carey's chickens[65] were constantly seen on the outward passage but none on my return. A shark was hooked and landed and did he not kick up a row till one of the sailors chopped off its tail with an axe.

On nearing New York a pilot came on board – sometimes they meet the ships two or three hundred miles from land. He was a very gentle looking man not a bit like a sailor in speech or appearance. At last we came in sight of land. The captain sent for me to come on the top of the round house to see a sight he said I never would see again unless I would come to New York again and oh what a magnificent sight, the whole coast for miles and miles seemed to be on fire.

When we got to the quay some priests met us and the boys who were not protestants went with them so there remained with me only seven who were protestants. What a busy scene there was on board that vessel but the most busy of all were boys who were buying up all the English halfpence and pence giving a cent for each which were disposed of in Canada at sixteen pence for every shilling. I may here say that English gold and Five pound notes are the only money that you get the full value – 4 dollars 84 cents for an English sovereign of Queen Victoria's reign. Less for older sovereigns. Any notes but English will scarcely pass at all. One poor Irishman had an Irish note. He came to me offering it for 15 shillings. He knew I intended going back. Well I gave him 20 shillings for it which pleased him not a little.

I had letters of recommendation from the Evangelical Protestant Alliance to three ministers, one a Doctor Cox a Presbyterian minister in Brooklyn, the second an Episcopalian, the third a Wesleyan. I saw very little of the two latter but Dr Cox and his wife [were] a dear couple. I attended his church which had a large Congregation but the only black man I saw in it was Dr Cox's servant. Dr Cox was a very eloquent sound gospel preacher. The last sermon I heard him preach was on the last verse of St Jude. There was a large Sunday school in connexion with the Church containing hundreds in which was one small class of black boys who sat just inside the school door, and there was but one teacher in the whole school who would teach them for one Sunday he being absent. He asked me to take his place for he said 'I know you wont mind'.

I saw some sights two of which I allude to. One the auctions held in the Bowery. The auctioneers employed talked so fast and loud that two hours were all the time they could stand it being completely worn out. The other in the meat market you could see the streets near the market shoals of well dressed men with baskets on their arms going for their meat and in less than five minutes all would be gone. It was in September and the weather was so hot that the meat would spoil if killed any length of time before being cooked. Another work was [*sic*] quite new to me was moving wooden houses in Brooklyn from street to street on great baulks of timber.

The eldest of my boys found a place for himself and another with the man who was the teacher of the little black boys. Recommended by Dr Cox. As the year was advancing and I being so much longer from home than I anticipated, being recommended by Dr Cox the remaining five boys were admitted into a Christian home and I at once started for Liverpool on board of the Constitution an American packet well fitted out for passengers. The passengers on board the Constitution were a very [?different] class from those in the Finland. Large numbers of gentlemen and ladies in the saloon one an American minister coming to Europe for the benefit of his health, more well to do people returning with money saved and a few when they found that they could not get money without hard labour were coming back to England with very little more than they brought out with them. The great majority of them were English, very few scotch and myself.

There was no communication between the saloon passengers and the second class than if half the Continent of the Great

Republic seperated [*sic*] them. Even when the minister held services on Sundays all of us were left out in the cold, but as I wrote to him telling him that we had souls as precious as the saloon ladies and gentlemen he very kindly came and conducted a service for us around the capstan. If there were any third class passengers on board I do not remember ever to have seen any of them as we second class were as aristocratic as the salooners.

Before going on board the Constitution I laid in a good and ample supply of provisions for the voyage and agreed with the Cook to cook for me. Some of my fellow passengers joined with me and the Cook cooked for us,[66] and as some had what others had not we had very palatable dinners so we lived well and enjoyed ourselves, and as the weather was cold we did not go on the deck very often so we did not see any of the officers or sailors only the third mate but more of him hereafter.

When we started for a few days the wind was favourable so the ship made good progress but the wind changed to the East and although the ship seemed to go ahead (no tacking or sail shifting) she made no progress as we were informed each morning by the little third mate. So things continued for a whole fortnight. [A]t last the mate came down to us with a smile on his face with the good news that the wind had changed. After the change of wind it was a grand sight to see the Constitution leaping through the water but she was far to the North and instead of sailing in by the South of Ireland the Captain took the northern Channel. We thought one day that we could see the Coast of Galway.

The Captain was an able sailor. [F]or that night, not being too sure where he was he backed the sails and laid too [*sic*] all the night, but as the day was breaking he got under sail (I was on board) and as the morning light increased we saw that we were running as straight as an arrow towards a most dangerous part of the Coast of Scotland. Such a shout to change sails was promptly obeyed so we soon entered the North Channel where we had Scotland on our left hand Ireland on our right. I scarcely left the deck all that day and was much pleased in passing the island of Rathlin to see the women hanging out their clothes to dry. When night came on it was a pleasant sight to see light after light on the Irish Coast.

Early next morning we were off the Isle of Man where a pilot was taken on board and so got into the Mersey early in the day but could not cross the bar till high tide as she wanted eighteen feet of water to cross the bar. Although a good dinner was being cooked for us, I and three others went ashore leaving our things and dinner in charge of our companions till Monday as we could not get through Custom House so late on Saturday. We went to a lodging house where one of the three men had lodged on his way to America, the landlady of which prepared for us a capital beef steak dinner and tea for which she charged us double. The dinner we enjoyed but not the double charge.

As soon as dinner was over contrary to my advice the three men went out to see the town the end of which was that two of them fell into the hands of some female sharks who robbed them of every penny they had, one even of his coat. The third man whom we called Big John (who was a fine specimen of a man) I found surrounded by prostitutes in a tavern who when they saw me fled. I brought him to our lodgings and as he wished to go seek the other two left in my keeping 400 golden guineas but did not find them.[67] One we called Leeds came back about midnight, the other a Scotchman early the next morning. I gave Big John back his 400 pounds telling him that he was a fool for trusting his money to almost a stranger. It was a pitiable sight to witness the scotchman's misery, his conscience pricked him so, he being a married man. That Saturday evening I caused my landlady to smile by asking her if she ever expected to see an Irishman who had more sense than two Englishmen and a Scotchman.

On Monday we soon got done with the Custom house officers but as the day was so very rough no boat ventured across the Irish Channel that night, but on Tuesday morning we started it still being very rough, so much so that the boat got no farther than Kingstown Harbour where she lay all night. Next morning we landed in Dublin and I got home that evening much to the joy of my wife and children as I had been more than five months from home.

I left Killina early in the year 1852 and went to my native parish to teach in Kilranalagh school where being badly paid[68] and having to work too much on some bad land which I had and my second [wife] dying there (as I have before stated),[69] I came to London in January 1858 and joined the London City Mission I passed 1857.[70]

The two living children of my second wife Jane, the first was a bright mite (she was born on the 23rd September 1849), came with me to London and in time grew up to be a woman, went to New Zealand in 1870 to her sister Elizabeth where she entered service but in a short time she married a Mr. John Smith a scotch farmer and as she came of farmer's descent she soon proved to him a good helpmate. They prospered well and would have done much better only for the overflowing of the Inch Clutha river which from time to time has caused them great loss.

Their children were six in number viz.

William born August 5th 1873
James born March 27th 1876
Jane born September 11th 1877
Robert born August 5th 1879 Drowned
Birdie born December 13th 1884
Jessie born July 31st 1889

Grandchildren. Jane's
Pearlie born September 15th 1898
Flossie born October 1903

My son Robert William's civil life proved a failure so he joined the Army when he was about 16 years of age. His corps was the C Battery of the Field Artillery. He served in several parts of England also in Bermuda and was sent out to South Africa and came in sight of the enemy immediately after Mr. Gladstone had concluded that ignoble peace after the disaster which befell our troops at Jehuba Hill.[71] He remained some time in South Africa and was with Sir Charles Warren when looking for Mr Bethel's body in Mehetabeland.[72]

While in England he was promoted to be sergeant and then joined the School of Gunnery in Shoeburyness where he made good progress coming out 2nd or 3rd out of 24. He was married while in Shoeburyness. He was then Sergeant Major. After his return from S. Africa he was at first stationed in Canterbury and then in Shornecliffe.

After full 20 years service with his Battery, still holding his connexion with his Battery, he was sent to Liverpool to organise and manage a Volunteer Battery there where he proved a great success being much prized by his Officers. Leaving Liverpool he joined the Royal Lancashire Yeomanry when her late Gracious Majesty gave him a Commission as Captain and he is doing duty now at the head quarters of the corps in Manchester as Captain and Quartermaster.[73]

Robert William Hanbidge married Miss Lawton in London. Their children:

Robert William born in Shoeburyness February 17th 1879
Eunice born in Shoeburyness April 17th 1880
Jane Frances born in S. Africa Decr. 13th 1884
Holly Susannah born in Shornecliffe December 10th 1886
William (dead) born in Liverpool February 10th 1889
Lewis Lancaster born in Liverpool April 13th 1890

Stanley born in Liverpool Jan. 7th 1892

Mary born in Liverpool June 11th 1899

Their Grandchildren

Robert William son of the above Robert William born in Liverpool 21 Ap. 1906

Son of Eunice born in Manchester 14th August 1906[74] her husband a Mr Ridgeway

MY LIFE AND WORK IN LONDON

I first came to London in December 1857 and on examination by some of the Committee and its secretaries of the London City Mission[75] I was appointed a missionary of the Society. I returned to Ireland to wind up my Irish affairs and got back to London about the middle of January 1858 and was appointed to a district in the parish of Christ Church Spitalfields. The Revd. John Patteson was my superintendent. The district was small in area but the population was large in number as there were upwards of 40 common lodging houses in the district. I found it one of the very worst districts in the East End of London as it was full of prostitutes, thieves, receivers of stolen goods &c. The thieves were numerous and day and night it was most unsafe for a stranger to pass through many of the streets of my district especially Flower and Dean Street in which I knew only three honest families.

While I was on the district I got 60 couples married who had been living together, one of whom was a grandmother, and I trust I did some good work among the fallen. I was well received amongst the lost ones, never was molested although a few times attempts were made to pick my pocket. Many meetings were held in the lodging houses by the missionary and other Christian workers on Sunday evenings so that much good seed was scattered but how much of it fell on good ground God only knows. I held a meeting once a week in George Street ragged school. The majority of those attending the school not born in wedlock. Their mothers took pleasure in sending them neat and clean.

After six years hard work I was removed to a district in White-chapel under the superintendency of the Revd James Cohen Rector of St Mary's Whitechapel. Before I was removed from Spitalfields I married a Miss Mary Ann Warren (who was a matron of a Home for training young girls for service)[76] on the 19th November 1862 who was a sincere Christian young woman and proved a good helpmate to me and a good mother to her two living children. More hereafter.

Only Brick Lane separated me from my other district but what a contrast between their people. Here there were only two lodging houses with respectable workmen in them, and in several of the courts there were clean honest industrious workmen with English wives from the country who kept their homes as clean as new pins. In Old Montague Street were three courts one all Irish the other two all English the first all dirt the other two the models of what cottages ought to be. There were some Jews and some Germans on the district one of the Jews an old eccentric lady said to me one day some of you Christeens (as she pronounced it) keep your Saviours birthday by getting drunk but she was honest enough to acknow-ledge that it did not apply to me.

In my visiting one day I went up stairs into a room to visit a young [woman] whom in my first week's mission work I saw in a court off of Fashion Street Spitalfields. My training superintendent recommended me to seek to get her into a home which I did into the Home where Miss M. A. Warren was matron. She turned out one of the most intractable girls that ever were at prayers; she would stop her ears like the deaf adder. I had not seen her for some time. When I began to speak to of Christ and salvation and need of it she cried out with a joyal [*sic*] voice Oh I am saved now and I found her hopes truly scriptural. My wife accompanied me next day to see her. She put her arms around her saying do not cease to teach the poor girls as you used to teach me for you do not know when good may be done. One of her sisters wanted to bring a priest to her. Her reply was Jesus Christ is my Priest.

I only staid about sixteen months in Whitechapel when the mission authorities removed me to the City of London and what a field of labour it was. The district was bounded on one side by Bishopsgate Street and Grace Church Street, on another side by Fenchurch Street and on the East side by Duke Street Bevis Marks and Camomile Street. It was a regular triangle containing part of seven or eight parishes but only five churches. Three synagogues. Very few of the people that I visited knew the parish they lived in and to have been visited by their minister they did not know who he was.

But what a field of labour was my district. Markets Meat, Poultry, Leather where were hundreds of men employed, Wine stores, Warehouses East and West Indies Billeter Street 6 or 7 floors, Cab ranks, Police on their beat, Housekeepers many living upstairs from 80 to 100 steps which was a labour to climb and more living downstairs several of them ladylike in manners and appearance and to them all I was a welcome visiter [*sic*]. A little girl called out one day Mamma here is the monthly messenger.[77]

A cabman said to me one day Sir we never see our children to talk with them for they are asleep when we go out in the morning and when we return at night.

I used to visit a large drug store in Leadenhall Street employing some scores of men. When the foreman first saw me [he] said I was the first man who ever visited them to ask them if they had a soul. The fruit market in Mitre Street Aldgate was a sad sight to be seen on Sunday mornings when hundreds of men came to buy oranges to hawk about in the streets all day long. The neglect of the Church towards the working men has been the cause of the alienation of the men from the church for while the clergymen of the Church of England visited but little the Nonconformist ministers visited none at all.

After eight years and six months missionary work in the City I removed to the district called St Luke's in a newly constituted Parish, parts of the parishes of St John at Hackney, St Barnabas Homerton, South Hackney Church and St Augustine Victoria Park, having the Revd W. H. Langhorne as my superintendent. I commenced visiting the above district about the middle of October 1872 where I worked 20 years and 2½ months when I was invalided and put on the disabled list after 36 years service. I visited every house in my district and every room in every house, all the shops and all the beer houses and some of the whiskey shops and was well received by all.

The most remarkable thing was that the whole district seemed to be a valley of dry bones. Still were a few who were bright christians living on the district and St Luke's Church used to be filled on Sunday evenings who came to hear Mr Langhorne preach, but very few belonged to the parish. Another portion of St John's Parish was added to St Luke's in which some of the members of St Luke's congregation lived. My work did not prove barren for some few did turn to the Lord with all their hearts.

My dear wife was struck with paralysis early in the autumn of 1879 and from that time till the 26th of May 1881 when she died she had very many attacks which greatly upset both her body and mind. She left two children Mary Ann born 3rd June 1866 and Henry Richard born 16th March 1868.

Mary Ann was a bright little girl from her very birth I may say. The first public school she attended was Homerton Row in Connexion with Homerton College.[78] (Congregational) and she made her mark among the little ones for when very young she wrote an essay of which the inspector said to the Head Mistress that he had been 16 years an inspector and he had never read anything to be compared with it. One of the Mr Buxtons[79] offered two scholarships of 30 pounds yearly for boys and girls under 13 yrs of age to be competed for by children in the schools of the North East and East End schools for which Mary Ann went in then being 11 years and three weeks of age which she won.

She then went to a junior school in Kentish town which was in connexion with Miss Buss's North London School for girls[80] where she always near (if not) the head of her class and the number of valuable books and other prizes which she won during her school career were not a few. At length she became head of the school and on leaving she was awarded two years free education in Bedford College. Next step was her matriculation in London University when she came out with honours. After one year's study she went in for her Intermediate examination and she came out head in the study of English for which she was awarded 60 pounds by the University and 60 pounds by the Gilchrist Trust for being second woman on the whole examination. The year following she was first for B.A. degree having left her rival of the year before a long way behind.

Miss Hanbidge then went to a Training seminary in Cambridge[81] and on leaving was engaged as assistant mistress at the ladies College in St Heliers Jersey where she continued for six years having made her mark as a successful classical teacher. From Jersey she removed to Cheltenham where Miss Beal[82] was head mistress and after two or three years having got a holiday she came home and studied for her M.A. degree[,] the upshot of which was that she came out first on the list at her examination. After her examination she went back to Cheltenham where she remained till she was appointed Head Mistress to a large secondary school[83] in Spital Square Bishopsgate Street without, which school has greatly prospered under her management. Proving that she is as able a teacher as she had been a pupil. So now she is a star of the First magnitude in the Educational world of our Great Metropolis. Her great memory and her indefatigable diligence have been causes in her great success.

Henry Richard my son also went to Homerton Row school at first among the infants and when seven years old went into the higher school. He made fair progress till he was 11 years of age when his health began to fail when I sent him to my brother's in Ireland where although he went to school for two years still it was lost time for he was taught but little. After his return to London he went to his old school but soon got a little place which through forgetfulness he did not keep so after some time he gave up all thoughts of looking for work and as I was getting old he looked after my safety. His health not being good at any time the doctor said he was suffering from Bright's disease. He turned his attention to astronomy and having got a telescope he looked at the sun for spots at the moon for craters and at numerous stars &c. Now he is a member of the British astronomical society whose meetings he attends monthly.[84]

CONCLUSION

I am come to the end of my autibiography [*sic*] being 93 years of age on the 16th April 1906.

I have said and done many things of which I am now ashamed.

But relying on God's promises I have accepted Jesus Christ's gracious invitation to come unto Him as a weary and heavy laden sinner and have found rest to my soul although the evil one tempts me to doubt. Wherefore I have put on the whole armour of God[85] that I may resist the wiles of the devil.

March 31st 1906

A Few Anecdotes of the Irish Rebellion of 1798
As I Heard From My Father

———————

It is a well known fact that Lord Edward Fitzgerald (a younger brother of the then Duke of Leinster) was the prime means of the Outbreak. The object being to establish a Republic in Ireland, and to this end there was established a society called the United Men which was joined by the Papists almost to a man also by many protestant churchmen and by the Presbyterians of the North of Ireland.

The first intimation my father had was from a near neighbour named Tom Hayden who asked him to join the United Men which he refused to do; so the following day he came and asked for the repayment of some money which he had lent him. Later in the spring of 1798 Hayden strove to persuade my father to give over planting potatoes saying that no one would ever dig them. The Haydens was quite a harmless family but evidently knew all about the conspiracy. When the outbreak took place they often saved my father's house from being burnt.

My grandfather had a servant boy (man) named Dwyer[1] who one day stuck his fack (spade) into the ground saying he would work no more. He started for Stratford on Slaney where a battle took place on that day (May or June). The rebels were attacked by Captain Saunders of Saunders' Grove and his Yeomenry[2] (all his tenants) who all being United Men fired over the rebels heads. The whole corps with their captain were marched into the Dunlavin town and were examined by some military commission and when asked confessed that they were united men (the Captain excepted) upon which they were shot on the fair green of Dunlavin one only escaped (named Pendergast [*sic*])[3] who was dangerously wounded he lay as if dead with his bowels protruding who got home somehow to his house where he lived a peaceful man for many years afterwards. Dwyer became a captain among them and was not at all bloodthirsty for many of the lives of the Co. Wicklow Protestants he saved.

There was a battle in Hacketstown[4] Co. Carlow where were a Corps of mounted Yeomenry who fled and hid under the bill [*sic*] of Eaglehill near to the town while the rebels killed a few protestants who were out in the town looking after their wives: others attacked a house used as a barracks, defended by Mr. Fenton and a Mr Finlay and their wives, all of Donoughmore Parish. While one of the ladies run bullets and the other loaded guns and blunderbusses while the men fired they were reduced to their last shot while the rebels were approaching the door covered with featherbeds[5] one of the ladies handed a blunderbus load to the mouth with all manner of missiles to Mr Finlay who fired it which cut a lane through the approaching rebels who lost heart and retreated.

That same day my father and a man called black Jem Plant were in hiding in fields on the banks of the river Slaney and as the evening was approaching they ventured up to house where they saw Mrs Plant[6] with her baby in her arms who intimated that the house was full of rebels on their retreat from Hacketstown[. T]hey burnt some houses the Glen of Imaal of united me[n] who fought against them that day in Hackesttown [sic] and would have burnt my father's house only for the Hayden family.[7] The rebels finally retreated to inaccessible parts of the Wicklow mountains and then part went down to the Co. Kildare where one of the leaders named Dalton (of whom my father often said he was a much braver man than Dwyer) was shot.

The rebellion took much greater root in the Co. Wexford than in any other part of Ireland for large numbers assembled on Vinegar Hill (near to the Town of Ferns) and formed a somewhat formidable camp. The camp on Vinegar Hill still held out so the Government ordered four divisions to march on it simultaneously and so attack on all sides at once: three of the divisions arrived in due time and commenced the attack at once. The rebels made but a feeble resistance and so sought safety in flight (after leaving many dead on the hill) and escaped as one of the commanders did not arrive in time. I suppose that it was so arranged by those in authority for Lord Cornwallis the then Lord Lieutenant of Ireland was a wise and merciful ruler. He called on the disheartened rebels to submit which thousands of them did[,] so he granted them letters of protection.

But although the rebellion was over, still a band led on by Captain Dwyer infested the parish of Donoughmore for some months hiding by day in the hills and as the yeomanry was constantly pursuing them they had to hide also by night. If they came across any very obnoxious person they killed him.

My father had an uncle named William Hanbidge who lived in Dublin who on his way to the country was taken by some of the marauders in Ballymore Eustace and by them marched to Blackditches hills and there killed. My father, having gone to live in Donard, from which he used to run up occasionally to Tinnahinch to see the place, was one day salting some pigs which he had killed was called on by Captain Heighington of Donard to pursue Dwyer and his gang who were seen passing between Fox Glen and the town. Captain Heighington gave the yoemen [*sic*] strict orders to make no noise nor to fire till they got near Dwyer and his men, instead of which some of his men when they got to the top of Donard Hill fired after them when they were almost half a mile behind, which only made Dwyer and his men run all the faster down Ballyvrain Mounroe Tinnah[8] across the river Slaney and so up the Glen of Imaal and so escaped. On the yoemen's [*sic*] way back they entered the house of a man Fitzpatrick nearly all of the men in it being dumb. Finding a soldiers uniform in it which some Dwyers men had thrown away in their flight they would have burned the house only my father persuaded them not to do so.

After crossing the Slaney on their way home they discovered a man hiding under the East bank of the river at whom several shots were fired, all of which missed him. He was arrested and turned out to be Antrim John a most notorious individual who had deserted from the Co. Antrim militia. He explained the meaning of some of his sayings. 'One a bad day I wouldn't meant a bad day he didn't kill some Protestant.' He pleaded with those in power that he was a loyal man but was led astray so he was allowed to join the army again but after a short time he began to tamper with other soldiers when he was shot without further trial. Some time after Antrim John's arrest, Dwyer and some of his men entered Tinnahinch house as my father and mother were at dinner when he said, So Mr Hanbidge you were out after me a few days ago; Yes said my father, and it was well for some of your friends as I saved their house from being burned. My father offered them something to eat which was refused, asked if there was a drop in the bottle which there was not, so they departed.

After playing hiding go seek a few weeks more Dwyer gave himself up to Mr Hume who made him some promises which the government refused to ratify. Mr Hume was surprised to learn from Dwyer that he knew so many things about Humewood. O, said Dwyer, Humewood was always noted for its hospitality, for he was oftentimes hid in Mr Hume's stables in the daytime and well entertained in the kitchen by the servants at night. Dwyer[9] was transported to Australia and Mr Hume was murdered in Carrick part of Kadeen Mountain. Lord E. Fitzgerald was shot in a house in Thomas Street Dublin.

A man named Finn who was taking care of Mr Greene's house when it was burnt was afterwards tried by court martial in Hacketstown as one of the incendiaries. My grandfather attended as a witness in his behalf for six days and on his evidence he was acquitted. The gratitude of the Finns ever afterwards the Hanbidge's was very much.

There were Hessian (called Hussians) soldiers in Ireland at the time whom everybody hated – the rebels because they were rebels and the loyalists because of their arrogance, avarice and impudence. One of them came to my father one day arrogantly demanding his mare to remove some soldiers baggage with terrible threats if he did not comply: Well, said my father, if you want her go and catch her: when he entered the field where the mare was she ran at him open mouthed, so Mr Hussian had to flee for his life. The rebels showed them no mercy when one of them fell into their hands. In the Co. Wexford it is reported that a rebel who was stripping one of them who had killed said to another who proposed to get part of the plunder, No go and kill a Hussian for yourself. The last sentence to this day is a Proverb among the people.

Matters Not Printed in the Main Body of 'Memories'

For Various Reasons: Religious, Political or Personal[1]

──────────

(*See page* 50) My brother Joe was I believe born lazy, at least he showed that he was very early in his life. So father used to say, 'I will give you a trade', consequently he was send to his Uncle Bob in Stratford to learn shoemaking. When he came home he began shoemaking for himself where he might have made a fortune if it had been diligent as he had nothing to pay for eating or lodging but it was not in his nature to be so. He married a nice young woman named Margaret Finlay and then went to live with her at her mother's but was always in want. He had three daughters, Eliza, Margaret and Kitty and a boy who died in babyhood. He often came home, especially on Sundays, but things always went ill with him.

He always loved me.

As shoemaking failed with him, he got into the Irish Constabulary and was stationed in the Co. Kildare near Dublin. But there things did not seem to go well with him for from his complaints he and his family were always on the verge of starvations. He left Kildare and joined the Dublin Police where they had to do police duty punctually night and day which caused his health to fail, so he had to resign and come back to his native parish where he lived a short time in a cottage in Whitestown thence to Kiltegan, Hackeststown [*sic*]. [H]is wife dying he married again and sunk, losing his second wife in the meantime till he entered Shillela poors house on a promise given him by the clergyman of Hacketstown that he would have his body brought and buried with his first wife in the church yard of that parish.[2] Thus the end of a lazy man, showing that a lazy tradesman wont succeed no more than a lazy farmer.

His eldest daughter Eliza was brought up at my father's for several years till she went to live in Hacketstown where she married a man scarcely half a remove from a savage. They had a large family and having left Hacketstown came to live in Donoughmore. The man worked some time for the farmers then for the Revd. Mr Townsend, the rector of Donoughmore, who soon removed to a parish near to Dublin where all the family followed, the growing up children soon got employment in a factory and all turned papists.

Next comes my eldest brother John[, who] was a diligent man at work but a very abusive one to his mother one to his mother [*sic*] and sister. Also most tyrannical to me and my young sister Kitty. I never knew him to abuse his father for the old man would not have put up with any of it: he was also kind to his other brothers for they were able to work. Kitty and I were not, so in his eyes we were incumbrances. He married a widow woman of Donard named Rainsford which for both parties turned out a very unhappy one. Both committed very grave faults. She had a farm which she strove to get a lease of in her own name so as to reduce him to be like a servant boy; also he was sued for her debts of which he knew nothing about until a writ was issued for his arrest. He to spite her turned libertine, following other women, so all happiness was at an end.

She died but he continued his libertine life till he was unable to keep the farm, so he gave up the farm to his brother Robert on condition that [it] should be kept but a very short time. He fell out with his sisterlaw [*sic*] and went to his brother Henry and worked on his farm but always grumbling and complaining and expecting and unreasonable things such as if any friend or friends came on an evening visit to his brother's he was to be called in for the feast. Things thus went on for two to three years till one day he tied up his legs with straw or hay ropes (to disgrace his brother) and went into Baltinglass poors house where he remained till the day of his death. He often came to see his brother especially if I were there but I always on my home visits called to see him and treated him more kindly than he did me in my early life. I have reason to hope that he was brought to look for pardon for all his sins through faith in Our Lord Jesus. He died in 1882 at the age of 84 years and his brother Henry buried him in Donoughmore church yard.

(*See page* 51) I must mention dear old Biddy Carpenter who was not too well used by my father's successor on the farm but was very poor and so was I at the time.

(*See page* 52) The Protestants of Donough [*sic*] had but little intercourse with their Romanist neighbours (my brothers had not) but one day I remember a meeting.

(*See page* 53) The first Hanbidges who came to Ireland with I think William the third prince of Orange and there have been Orangemen in their family from that time to this. I myself was secretary to an Orange lodge and attended orange lodges in London some years ago.

(*See page* 54) John when he grew up joined the Irish Constabury [*sic*] but after a few years he came to London and entered the London Metropolitan Police which he soon had to leave through misconduct which undermined his health and from that time to now (for he is still alive over 70 years of age) he has gradually sunk and sunk (Beer much helping his downfall) till as a fisort [*sic*] he had to enter the Hackney Union constantly grumbling, blaming everybody but himself, forgetting that whatsoever man soweth that must he reap.

William came to London and was employed in the General Post Office where he could have done, only drink was his downfall. He had to resign and went to America but he returned to England and after a time went to America again and joined a whaling expedition to Artic regions. He fell out with some of the officers so he left and came back to London now a trained sailor, went some voyages to the far east in good seaworthy healthy ships and on his last voyage (having fallen out with the mate) he joined a coasting vessel where the bad water almost poisoned him then being entirely upset he was sent home by one of our consuls and when was landed in Southampton he made his way to London and got into St. George's Hospital where he died a victim to his own acts. His death took place on the 23rd February 1876. Buried in Abney Park Cemetry [*sic*].

(*See page* 55) Thus ends the history of my family by Anna Rosetta Hocter proving that sins never pays [*sic*] even in this life.

(*Note.* – Many eugenists hold that consumption in a mother is sometimes followed by alcoholism in her sons. M.H.)

(*See page* 59) When we got to the quay some Romish priests met us and persuaded the boys who were Romanists to go with them so there remained with me only seven who were protestants. The priests asked for money which they did not get.

(*See page* 62) The majority of the fallen women were from Cork, for a few years before (a short time after the Irish famine) the Cork steam packet companies fell out and in consequence great numbers of Cork girls got over to England for one shilling each. Consequently as they could not get into service multitudes took to the streets and they proved a terror to every place where they were; drunkenness making them worse and notwithstanding all they prided themselves in being holy Catholics.

The Rebellion

(*See page* 71) Lord Cornwallis the then Lord Lieutenant of Ireland was a wise and merciful ruler. He called on the disheartened rebels to submit, which thousands of them did so he granted them letters of protection but in the meantime a deadly warfare was carried on between the Yeomanry and roving bands of popish rebels when many of both sides were slain even some of those who had Lord Cornwallis' protection. For instance some yeomanry met a man who had a protection near to Donoughmore church who bragged that he had burnt George Fenton's house in Knockinargen, and Fenton, who was one of the yeomen, shot him and left him in his agony on the road side to die, all afraid to render him help. Fenton had to fly to some friends in the Co. Wexford where [he] remained some time.

(*See page* 72) A wounded rebel took refuge with a Mrs Valentine at the entrance to Saunders' Grove who was loved by Mrs Valentine who proposed to elope with him, but as he had a sweetheart he refused so in refenge she informed on him when he was taken and shot. A few nights afterwards she was fearfully mutulated [*sic*] and murdered.

Mary Ann Hanbidge's Contributions

✶

Introduction (1939)

My Father William Hanbidge, schoolmaster and London City Missionary, was the tenth child of John Hanbidge farmer, of Tinnahinch, County Wicklow, Ireland. He was born in 1813 and died in 1909.

In his ninety-third year at my request he put into writing some memories of his life, which are now printed in this book dedicated to his memory. At first he wrote 'Thoughts of my Young Days' only; but I asked him to tell us much more, so that his book gradually developed into an autobiography, written in two overlapping parts. He wrote it in a few months with no notes to help him except a few dates of marriages, births and deaths. It is printed exactly as he wrote it; spelling, punctuation and capitals, paragraphs and divisions are his; nothing is altered, but there are one or two omissions of matters which he wrote for his children only, with no thought of publication.

I am indebted to my cousins for information they have given me, to John Hanbidge of Dunlavin, the Rev. Alfred Hanbidge of Dundalk and his father John of Ballintruer, Sarah Hanbidge of Stratford, Henry and Kathleen Hanbidge of Talbotstown,

Catherine Scanlon and Edward Jones grandchildren of Tinnahinch. I know that for them, as for myself, such work was a labour of love. I have also to acknowledge with grateful thanks help received from many quarters: from T. U. Sadleir, Esq., Office of Ulster King of Arms, the Rev. F. F. Empey, Rector of Donoughmore, Canon Hodges, Principal of Kildare Place Training College, His Honour Justice Liam Price, the Rev. Chancellor J. B. Leslie; from the National Library and the Public Record Office of Ireland; from the Public Librarian of Gloucester, the Editor of the *Wilts and Gloucestershire Standard*, the Secretary of the Royal United Service Institute, the Secretary of the London City Mission, Mr Winston, Senior Warden of the Weavers' Company of Cirencester, and Mr Brian Frith, genealogist, of Gloucester.

Mary Hanbidge, 1939.

MY FATHER

To my parents I owe everything. My Mother died when I was a child; my Father lived to the age of ninety-six, an abiding influence. He was above all things a Man, and a good man, 'strong and very courageous'. My brother Robert, soldier and judge of men, told me he had never seen him afraid or heard him tell a lie. He had intellect and common-sense, genial humour and original wit quite free from malice; he had strength of mind of body and of principle. He loved his children dearly, and not least dearly the two children of his older years, his 'English edition' as he used to call us; he gave us all that he had, and the chances that he never had.

His life was hard. He told me once he used to wonder why the gentlemen did not grow up soft till he saw them playing games in Trinity College grounds and then he understood. In Ireland and for many years in England he was seldom free from domestic and never free from money worries; and as an Irish country national schoolmaster in the thirties and forties of the nineteenth century his intellectual life was narrow and circumscribed by class, with few books or friends of his mental stature; but he was of a buoyant frame of mind, he loved his parents, his brothers and the home where he was born, whilst the Bible which he knew through and through opened to him great literature and wide horizons which never failed him.

He had a hard upbringing; and he brought us up very strictly. On Sunday we went to Church morning and evening and to the Wesleyan Sunday School in the afternoon; he thought we should learn more of the Bible there than at St Luke's. Our only books on Sunday were 'Peep of Day' and Bible Stories, and as we grew older the big illustrated Bible and an illustrated *Foxe's Book of Martyrs*; if we wanted to go anywhere on Sunday, the Sabbath, we had to walk. We had Family Prayers every morning and evening and always Grace at meals. I read no novels or plays and never went to parties or to the theatre till school began little by little to give a wider outlook. It was a Puritan upbringing; but looking back on it, I do not know of a better one in our circumstances; it had a dignity and a stability of its own.

His old home drew him back from England whenever it was possible, at first about every fifth year, and more often afterwards. At first, not understanding London ways he used to walk from Whitechapel to Euston to ask about the trains to Liverpool, but later on he found out about time-tables. He and I went to Ireland ten times from 1882 to 1903, his last visit was in 1904. Though he lived in London fifty-one years he never lost his Irish tongue, and when he was over ninety and had been buying plants in Farringdon Street market he asked me 'How do they know I am an Irishman?' To the end his tiny London garden satisfied in its tiny way his innate love of the soil; and he had his Bible and many friends.

He followed my work at School and College with joy; later on was a constant visitor at the Central Foundation School, where everybody loved him. His last visit there was in the May of the year he died, and a girl who saw him only that once said to me recently, 'I have never forgotten that dear old man'. At the presentation made to me when I retired in 1929 I spoke of what I owed to my Father; and an old pupil, who had left nearly thirty years before, said to me afterwards 'I was waiting for you to say that': so strong was the impression he had made at eighty-eight on a growing girl.

In his work as a London City Missionary he had the same abiding influence. A Secretary of the Mission wrote to me in 1938:

20 July 1938

My memory of his delightful personality and charm is as vivid as ever. I shall never forget my first meeting with Mr Hanbidge. It was on the terrace of the London City Mission Home at Ventnor, about 1891. There were three Irishmen together exchanging confidences and badinage. Mr Hanbidge excelled all in his racy humour and quaint stories. I was a young man then, freshly entered upon my life's work in the Mission. Mr Hanbidge was many years my senior, but his kindly, gracious manner, his fund of anecdote, always apropos of the subject of conversation, and ever indicating the loving tender spirit of a good man, completely won my heart. I am an old man myself now, but in my forty-nine years of service in the Mission, thirty-two as one of its secretaries, I never met a man who more impressed me as a true Christian gentleman, one who brought to the service of his Master gifts of wit and wisdom, always full of fun and vitality, but never unkind in his judgment, a true loyal witness for his Lord.

It was my first meeting with an Irish Protestant. All my early opinions of this type of man had been frankly critical, almost hostile. I regarded him as a man who delighted in the expression by word and deed of violent, bigoted propaganda. I know him better now. I have had many Irish friends and comrades since those days, but the first and best remembered was dear old Mr Hanbidge. 'He being dead yet speaketh.'

In every company shouts of laughter used to greet the tales he told. In his ninety-fifth year he was apparently dying; the doctor fetched at 3 a.m. administered strychnine as a forlorn hope. Called back from the gates of death he opened his eyes and feebly greeted his friend and doctor watching at the foot of his bed with a funny tale about an Irishman; finding it was not appreciated as was usual, he repeated it. 'Upon my soul', said the astonished doctor, beating on the bed in his surprise, 'that man has as many lives as a cat!'

But two years later his time had come. A month before he died he went to Church in his bath chair for the last time; then he began to slip away; gently and painlessly he faded, he was in bed ten days only. Five days before he died as I read to him the twenty-third Psalm, he repeated audibly the words 'Surely goodness and mercy have followed me all the days of my life, and I will dwell in the house of the Lord for ever.' They were his last words, save for a faintly murmured 'Dear Daughter' nearer the end. He died on Wednesday 22 September 1909. A pious Jew who admired him spoke a fitting epitaph, 'Miss Hanbidge, if your father had not lived like that he would not have died like that.'

MY FATHER'S HOME

The homestead of Tinnahinch stands far back from the road down Kelsha Hill; a long lane, just wide enough for a cart, leads to the yard. Outside the upper gate is the opening to the haggard with its stone supports for ricks. Inside the gate is the new well; and on the left the house itself with the fowl-houses and cow houses; on the right the car house for ass's car, gig, etc., the barn and the dairy. Beside the dairy three stone steps lead up to the garden with its gooseberry and currant bushes, cabbages, lilies, stocks and roses. Beside the lower gate is a shed for carts and just outside the yard the pig-styes; the bull's house is now at the back of the house on the site of the bacon curing sheds burnt down in 1798. Behind the house is the row of poplars planted by my grandfather; there are tall elms in all the hedgerows.

The path from the lower gate is bordered by a ditch and hedge in which a quern (old stone hand-mill) is hidden; it goes through the dunghill field to the brook, and thence on one side over the Big Bank to the big river meadow and the Slaney, and on the other to the moor, whence every evening the cows come home for milking at the call 'Bail up! Bail up!'

From the Big Bank and the garden you can see the full breadth and almost all the length of the wide Glen of Imaal, walled in by its mountains: Keadeen, 'the flat-topped', over two thousand feet high, and the great Gap and then the third highest in all Ireland, Lugnaquillia, three thousand feet and more with its mighty 'Prisons', and the old military road leading over the Black Banks to Glen Malure, Church Mountain with its memories of ancient days, Fauna across the moor blocking the view to Donard, Davidstown Chapel clear against the sunset, Kilranalagh Hill and Brusselstown, Slaney and Little Slaney in rain foaming down the sides of 'Lug' and winding their way brown and boulder strewn across the wide expanse of moor and meadow and wood.

For us the centre of that lovely scene has always been the little house of Tinnahinch, the House of the River Meadow, the home of my grandparents. My grandfather built it about 1795, a thatched one storey house of three rooms, 'the room' (i.e. the large end room, where all the children were born), the kitchen and the small bedroom. It must have been a tight fit as the family grew; so afterwards a loft, reached by a movable ladder, was made under the roof above the small bedroom.

Elsewhere there was no ceiling, only the roof; boughs of trees supported the thatch, black with age and turf smoke, two or three deer's antlers hanging from it. I saw it like that in 1882 and later, but I did not see my aunt as she sat spinning with homemade rushlights the only light, for that was the work of winter nights when she was younger. Many things have changed about the house. Beyond 'the room' there is another large room where the bull's house used to be; a ceiling of pitch pine planks, itself now black with smoke, follows the slope of the thatched roof and hides it; the outer walls are grey with cement not gleaming with whitewash now; the roof is iron not thatch; but the great fireplace is still there where you can sit on benches beside the hearth fire right under the chimney and see the sky above you; the tiny cupboard for salt (salt was so dear) is in the wall beside the fire; the long movable irons hang from the crossbar, with their hooks for the three legged pots which swing over the fire heaped on the great stone hearth, coke, and turf when they can get it; and soda bread and potato cakes are still baked in the flat round iron vessel set on the hearthstone with the glowing coals heaped round it and on the cover. So had they cooked on the Irish hearths from time beyond memory and so my grandmother baked her cakes. Outside the fireplace is the long high-backed settle with a chest running under the whole length of the seat, the tall cornbin with sloping lid, the little shelves on the wall for spoons and mugs, the dresser with big shelves for crockery and spaces underneath which covers almost all the end wall, and under the little deep-set window the big deal table where the serving men eat; they sit on long four-legged deal stools, scrubbed like the table white with river sand. The master's large wooden armchair stands in front of the hearth: it was my Father's seat in the later years. There are wooden chairs for others, and the whole life of the house has its centre in the kitchen.

When my grandparents settled at Tinnahinch it was a holding of twenty acres only. Close by a widow had a cottage in 'Hal's Acre', now the night field; she and the Tinnahinch folk shared the spring there. The Haydens had another holding nearer the Slaney, with the other well. Both these holdings were afterwards joined to Tinnahinch, and for over a hundred years every drop of water for the house was carried from the Haydens' spring, down by the river bank a quarter of a mile away. (The water for the animals and for cleaning came from the brook, and there was a small supply of rainwater.) This heavy labour ceased only a few years ago when a well was sunk in the yard by the house. Tinnahinch has known changes in its roof, its walls, its rooms and its fields; but still it is Tinnahinch.

Folklore and Superstitions (1938)

─────────

These were mostly told me by my cousins in 1938.

On Easter Sunday morning people got up early to see the sun dance. One May Day, very early in the morning, farmers would plant twigs of the quicken tree, the mountain ash, all about their pastures to keep the witches 'the bad people' from casting a spell on their cows so that they gave no milk during the year. On May Day also it was unlucky to give or lend anything whatever out of the house to a neighbour, milk, utensils, etc. The worst thing to give was a glowing turf to revive a fire; that gave the borrower power to lay a spell on cattle.

It was unlucky to give the stalled cattle food between Old Christmas Day and New Christmas Day, so the mangers in the sheds were made large enough to take the full supply of food for the twelve days. The mangers in some of the farms are still very large, but the superstition which began with the change in the Calendar has died out.

Spells on cattle were greatly dreaded. Sometimes 'the bad people' would churn with an empty churn as their neighbour's cows came home for milking, and there would be no butter when the milk was churned. But there were remedies. If the butter would not come, the butter-makers put quicken twigs round the churn and sometimes struck the cows in the cowhouse with a quicken gad (gad is found in Shakespeare, it is a spike, a wand or road, like goad); or they put a pinch of salt in the churn; or they put plough irons round the churn, touching it. (Compare Rudyard Kipling's 'Cold Iron').

Once Jane of Ballintruer was going to bring in a cow when she saw some people boiling a kettle with paper put under the lid. She said 'You won't have the whole of it!' and snatched the paper away. For a year that cow gave milk to Jane only. Friendly people who came in while churning was going on would say 'God bless the work'; and take a turn at the churn to show they had no evil intentions.

It was unlucky to meet on the road a red-haired woman or girl, a man with a squint, or two magpies; you must turn back at once. It was unlucky for two members of a family to be married on the same day.

In horse racing, threshing (with four or six horses), churning with a machine worked by an animal, everything moved clockwise, in the path of the sun. It was unlucky to go widdershins, i.e., against the path of the sun.

It was most unlucky to destroy a rath, or to cut down white-thorn trees growing beside one. Many years after Mr Greene's struggle with evil powers a neighbour of Tinnahinch took men to cart away a small rath close to the Tinnahinch boundary.[1] When his men came back to him from their dinner he stopped the digging, a silent and a broken man who told no man that day or ever after what he had seen. The rath cut in half is still there. (A rath is a prehistoric mount, defensive or sepulchral.)

There are many other stories about moats, raths, and Danes' castles. Here are two, one about Ballintruer and one about Donard:

About 1750 a local man, Doyle of Stratford, dreamt three nights in succession that if he went to the Danes' Castle by Ballintruer in the night time and dug a hole in the floor, he would find a chest of gold. Two conditions must be strictly observed; first, no one of the party was to speak a word until the gold was found; and secondly, he was to take a live cock with him and kill it when he had found the gold. A party was made up; they went to the old castle and dug the hole four feet down; when the man that was using the fack (spade) hit an iron box he gave a great shout with an oath; straightway the fack fell from his hand and the iron box receded from him. In great fright they all ran away. Next day a neighbour went to see the hole; he found a large lump of gold worth several pounds.

The cousin who told me this tale at the age of seventy-seven is a son of Ballintruer. He added 'It would seem that the Danes had the best of the fight for the chest of gold.'

I saw the old Castle this year, 1938. Part of one side wall is standing and one gable end; the standing walls are about twelve feet high and three and a half feet thick. The hole in the centre of the floor is still there; it is about four feet by two and a half; for it has been partly filled in, as a cow fell into it and got hurt. There is also a hollow in the ground all round the castle like a dyke, where water was let in from the stream near by. Ballintruer means 'the house of the stream'.

The story about the Ball Moat at Donard is similar. There they did not dare to begin digging till a life was taken on the spot; so they killed a cock on the top of the Moat. When they had dug down about six feet a black bull leaped forth from the opening and the assembled people fled in terror.

Water in the hollows of ancient stones never dries up, and is a cure for warts, sore eyes, etc. Justice Price tells me that such stones are often called bullan stones, bull·n means a round hollow; the holes were used for grinding corn or pounding vegetables. Bullan stones are particularly common in the district round Glendalough. There are three such stones at the foot of the rath near the Tinnahinch boundary. One is a large worked granite boulder, 18 by 33 inches with its levelled top surface about 36 inches above the ground; there are three round holes in it, 16 ½ , 13 and 13 ¾ inches across respectively and about 5 inches deep. The other two stones are boulders levelled on the surface only; each has one hole about 13 inches across and 5 inches deep.

The Banshee used to wail round Ballintruer.

My father told me that the Glen folk used to pass newborn children through dung. The use of dung as a disinfecting medicament is folklore, not a mere superstition. The Arabs use it as a poultice for boils, etc., and it is so used in Guernsey, where an old farmer's wife once said to the head of the Guernsey Ladies' College 'There is nothing like a good clean cow's dung poultice for carbuncles.' A dung poultice is regularly used in Ireland for cows and oxen and for horses' sore feet; people say that the green herbs on which the cattle feed give virtue to the dung.

There are other old time healing agents that are still in use. Dock roots boiled in ale are one cure for jaundice. Another made by healers of great repute is not very alluring, but is said to be very efficacious and to succeed where more orthodox methods fail. It consists of fat earth worms boiled in milk; the worms are well washed and put into a muslin bag before the boiling, which produces a thick oily liquid. In the mountain village outside the Glen lives a famous healer, the son of a healer, who is well known for his treatment of jaundice. The country people say 'There is one sort of jaundice which the doctor can cure, and one which the doctor and the healer can cure and one which only the healer can cure.' At any rate this man can even cure jaundice in dogs. A story goes round that a doctor was very ill with jaundice, and at last he said 'It is quite unprofessional, but I am going to the healer'; and he was cured; whilst another being urged to go said 'It is impossible for me to go.' His adviser said 'It is not impossible for you to die.' He did die. I do not vouch for the truth of these stories, but people believe them. They believe also that this man can cure external cancer. I know that this is said to be utterly impossible; but I know also some one who three years ago was suffering agony from an external growth of some kind; and under his treatment, which for six months she had refused to try, it has disappeared; and she is well.

My cousin, Mrs Henry Hanbidge of Talbotstown, has a recipe for ointments, very old and very good. It involves much hard work. For burns and skin treatment generally you gather in June the leaves of the following plants, about two pounds of each; ivy, plantain, hart's tongue fern and the young tips of elder shoots. Cut them up very small and put them in a pan with two pounds of unsalted butter; simmer on a slow fire until it is a good green colour; this takes about three hours. When it is cool enough, squeeze out with the hand the ointment, i.e., all the grease and juice, leaving in the pan only a solid mass of withered herbs. With butter it is for human use; if made with lard, for animal use.

For blasts and other sores use the leaves of plantain, hart's tongue fern, the young tips of elder, forum, ribgrass, ragweed, chicken weed, groundsel, tansy, yarrow, marsh mallow, crowfoot, foxglove, laurel, and daisy roots. Proceed as above, but use four or five pounds of butter, Again, you can use lard for animal use; but if made with butter it is twice as strong, because of the herbs the cows themselves fed on. It is especially efficacious in the treatment of inflamed udders in cows. The ointment is of a deep green colour, like germolene and palm olive soap, only darker. It will last a full year till the herbs come again. The recipe has been handed down at Ballintruer at least since the time of Long Anne; but it is far older than that. Lady Wilde in her book *Ancient Cures, Charms and Usages of Ireland* (1890) speaks of an ancient cure, a green ointment, 'which in the hands of a wise woman is very efficacious'.

Notes

WILLIAM HANBIDGE'S MEMORIES

A FEW THOUGHTS OF MY YOUNG DAYS

1 My Father took 29 May for his birthday. In 1893, his brother Henry said that he was with the men planting potatoes on the moor when a message came from the house that a boy was born. Potatoes were planted in the middle of April.

2 'She took it from me by force'.

3 Biddy Carpenter 'was my champion on all occasions and fought all my battles'.

4 '1817. Being a year of Scarcity Revd. Sir Saml. Synge Hutchinson gave £100 to buy provisions for distressed persons resident on his Estates in this Parish.' (Record of Donations and Bequests).

5 No doubt they called them 'crickawns', the Anglicised form of the Irish word for a small hill and a little potato.

6 That big stone is still in the meadow by the Slaney. One of the cows was a little black Kerry, an excellent milker, that my Father loved.

7 There was no Poor Law in Ireland until after 1838. Arthur Moore's *List of Poor Law Unions 1847* states that the Baltinglass Union consists of the following parishes – Baltinglass, Stratford, Kiltegan, Rathdangan, Donoughmore, Donard, Dunlavin, etc.

8 Knockanarrigan is a hamlet with a shop, about two miles away. He always went barefoot; when he was a grown lad he used to carry his shoes if he were going to Church, etc., and put them on when he got near.

9 The top of the Big Bank is one of the measuring points of the Ordnance Survey, 584 feet high. When a survey was being made in the nineteenth century someone asked the men on the Big Bank with their instruments what they were doing. They said 'Half an acre of land has been lost in Ireland and we are looking for it'. Finding that truth did not live on the top of the Bank, the inquirer went away.

10 Donoughmore is about a mile and a half, Davidstown Chapel half a mile, and 'my grandfather's' (Ballintruer) three miles distant from Tinnahinch; 'my uncle's' (Ballyreisk) is only just across the Slaney.

11 Kelsha and Gibstown Bridges are over the Slaney. The blind arch is over a very deep pool separated from the river.

12 These were technical terms for the following processes:

   (a) Broke with a brake: the stalks of the flax were crushed with the proper tool.

   (b) Skutched: the seeds were beaten out, I suppose with a flail. The same word was used for the separation of grains of corn from the husk.

   (c) Carded: a thin wooden board with a handle attached was pierced with steel wire, as fine as a fine sewing needle. The wire was fastened at the back and cut at the top so that the board was studded with tiny points, or hackles, of sharp wire each about a quarter of an inch long, arranged in rows. The flattened stalks of the flax were drawn backwards and forwards over the points till the fibres were combed out, thin and straight. The board was about one and a half feet square or sometimes only the size of an octavo book. John, grandson of Edward and Mary Molyneux, told me that when he was a little boy at Ballintruer he used to see an old woman carding wool fibres in the same way she earned her living by carding for the farmers' wives. My grandmother did it for herself.

13 Long after my Father's day, on the cross road from Kelsha Hill to Davidstown Chapel there was a little hamlet of about twenty families, a small colony of weavers who wove blankets and linen for the countryside. Jack Flynn must have lived there and no doubt the Ned Flynn who inoculated my Father for the smallpox. This small holding, 'German Flynn's', was bought by my Uncle Edward of Tinnahinch some time before 1876. A path to the ruins of the houses still runs from the road and the well is there. The Donoughmore Parish Register mentions a George Flynn of Kelsha in 1762, and Flynns still hold the surrounding land.

14 Billy Boy used to wind the warp which had two twists; his mother wound the weft. They used to wind it very tight indeed to squeeze out the natural oil. He told me this when I said he was winding my knitting wool much too tight. A tuckmill had machinery for pressing the oil out from the woven woollen fabric. There is an ancient place called Tuckmill near Baltinglass.

15 Compare the Scottish plaids.

16 He used to travel to Dublin by the coach road with his waggon of bacon once a week. He took to market sides, shoulders and hams. The fall of the pig was what was not sent to market, i.e. head, tail, trotters, offal, lard. This is what my Father calls 'pig's meat'.

17 My English grandfather, Richard Warren, born in 1794, told me that the labouring people in East Anglia at first refused to use the new earthenware plates in place of wooden trenchers and pewter, because they thought they would turn the edges of the knives. I have not heard this about Ireland.

18 Also there was plenty of cabbage, but winter greens were unknown in Tinnahinch till my Father introduced them, I think, about 1840 from Carlow. When times were bad they had another dish, 'potatoes and point': they ate the potatoes and pointed at the bacon. Sometimes pedlars hawked barrels of Dublin Bay herrings round the Glen.

19 Of course she used the old 'dolly' churn. When I was a girl visiting at Tinnahinch they had a 'contraption' to lessen the labour; in the garden behind the dairy an ass turned a large iron wheel with a ord attached which passed through a hole in the wall and worked the churn. The ass walked clockwise, i.e. following the path of the sun.

20 For clarity's sake, I have placed quotation marks round what I take to be the offensive phrase, without knowing wherein the offence lay (W. J. Mc C.).

21 By contrast, the farms and cottages were all thatched.

22 'When I found I had no brother Bob with me I cried all day long, so next morning I told father I would go to school.'

23 The system in force in Mr Iver's hedge school in Davidstown was a primitive form of the Dalton system, which the United States has discovered so recently. You were told what to do; you did it by yourself. Class teaching, always necessitated by scarcity of books, became more practicable when Bell and Lancaster introduced the monitorial system. Originally a hedge school was a school held in the open air under a hedge; later a sort of rough shed was made. The hedge schools of Celtic Ireland in the eighteenth century produced many fine classical scholars. In 1570, the twelfth year of Elizabeth, an Act of Parliament enacted 'that there should be henceforth a free school within every diocese of the realm of Ireland'; but one free school in the diocese of Dublin did nothing to help the Glen.

24 Erasmus Smith (1611–91), the son of Sir Roger Smith of Husbands Bosworth, was a Turkey merchant and a member of the Grocers' Company. In 1650 he appears in the State Papers as an army contractor supplying large quantities of oatmeal, wheat and cheese for the troops in Ireland and Scotland. Under the confiscating acts of 1642 he was an adventurer of £300 towards prosecuting the war against the insurgents of 1641; at the Cromwellian settlement of 1652 he received 600 acres of land in County Tipperary; and by 1684 he held 46,449 acres in nine counties. He early projected a scheme for the education of children on his estates 'in the fear of God and good literature and to speak the English tongue'. By indenture of 1 December 1657, he founded five grammar schools having bursaries at Trinity College, Dublin, and five elementary schools, under eighteen trustees including five nonconformist divines (Independents); the children were to be taught the Assembly's catechism. By an Act of 1723, the Governors established the 'English Schools'; most of these schools were started between 1801 and 1823. In their day these English Schools did a great work for education, and many of the teachers brought their schools to a high state of efficiency. 'In 1821 Lord Wicklow granted half an acre of Ground on which to erect the Parish School House' (Record of Donations and Bequests to the Parish of Donoughmore); and I suppose Squire Greene gave the land for the Kilranalagh School. When the National Board was established it gradually took over the English Schools.

25 In 1812 there were less than 5,000 schools of all descriptions in Ireland, and most of those miserably poor; they were housed in mud-floored cabins, sometimes without chimneys or even windows, without desks, without seats except stones or sods. The teachers who were sometimes nearly paupers aimed at teaching only reading, writing and arithmetic. The books for reading were generally supplied by the pupils, and were sometimes very undesirable. There was universal lack of discipline. To remedy this state of affairs the Society for Promoting the Education of the Poor of Ireland was founded in December 1811. At this time in Great Britain, Dr Andrew Bell was founding the National School Society and Joseph Lancaster the British and Foreign School Society.

The Irish Society began the first piece of its work, the Training School for masters, in a house in St James' Parish. By 1814 they were training teachers and publishing books for use in the schools, first of all a Spelling and a Reading Book, to be followed later by works on Arithmetic, Needlework, Geography, Geometry, Trigonometry, and Mechanics, a Schoolmaster's Manual, and sets of 'Cheap Books' for their school libraries.

In 1815 Parliament voted a grant of £6,980 for the building of a Training School and a Model School in Kildare Place, whence the Society became known as the Kildare Place Society. England had to wait until after the Reform Act for any grant from Parliament for national education.

In Kildare Place Model School there were 700 or 800 pupils and in the Training School as time went on about 150 men and, after 1824, 60 women were trained each year. The normal course of training lasted for six weeks; weak students might remain for three or even four months. In 1830 the Society was responsible for 1,636 schools. This work was carried on in an undenominational spirit and (*mirabile dictu* for the time and the country) there was no attempt at proselytising; only simple Bible reading without note or comment was insisted on.

At first the work was approved by all creeds and parties in Ireland, was supported by the British Parliament, and was admired in many European countries; but by 1819 attacks began to be made on the system of Bible Reading, which the Society refused to alter; and in 1831 Parliament withdrew its grant. In 1854 the Kildare Place Training College had passed into the hands of the Church Educational Society, and in 1878 the General Synod of the Church of Ireland assumed responsibility and renamed it the Church of Ireland Training College. In 1937 thirty students were in training.

When my Father speaks of Kildare Street Training School, not Kildare Place, he is not incorrect. His wife was in the Mistresses' Department which in 1824 was built opening on to Kildare Street. In his criticism of its work I think perhaps he was not thinking it as an institution giving a short course of training for teachers but was comparing it with his own Training School, which was practically a secondary school.

26 Possibly this was the first generation to be regularly taught reading and writing. The Donoughmore Vestry Books (1794 onwards) show that my great grandfather and his

brothers and my grandfather and his brothers could write, so no doubt they could read. My grandfather had a good mathematical brain, as Father had, and at market he could sum up the weight and money value of a bullock at sight, whether he could read and write or no. His children were taught to spell words of seven syllables before they were taught to read.

27 The Reverend Thomas Francis Greene, Curate of Donoughmore, was the son of Lawyer William Francis Greene, squire of Kilranalagh. He became Curate in April 1819, aged twenty-nine. My Father told me that the Parish was heathen till he came to it: 'there was no knowledge of anything, but all manner of superstitions'.

Apparently no one did much to help the Glen. Mostly the Parish stood on its own feet, and the gentlemen farmers (Fentons, Higginbothams, Valentines, etc.) with the small farmers did their best by it, as the Vestry Books show.

The Revd. Joseph Tenison was Curate from 1801 until his death in February 1808, and 'Isham Baggs' presides at the Vestry in May 1808. Baggs later became a 'Couple-Beggar', i.e., he celebrated clandestine marriages cheaply as a free lance. Dr Edward Ryan, Prebendary and Rector from 1795, took over the Parish in 1809 (possibly he was tired of curates), and then things were different. My Father's summing up gives the state of the Parish as it appeared to the opening mind of an intelligent boy. 'There was no knowledge of anything but all manner of superstitions.' The curate Reverend Mr Greene made my Father's life intellectually and spiritually, and 'Memories' bears witness to his devoted work. To my Father's mind he was 'the best man that ever lived', and he remembered with delight his commonsense and wit. 'What a cock-and-bull story!' was his comment on the Sadducees' tale of the seven brothers. I think one of his greatest achievements was inducing his father to teach the children; and he himself tried to teach the grown-ups other things besides religion. For instance, he waged unceasing war on the practice of keeping dunghills beside the door till one day his horse stumbled and flung him head first into one. 'It saved his neck and he never spoke a word against a dunghill after.'

28 The Plant family were sextons of Donoughmore from 1818 to 1910; first the brothers Robert and Thomas joint sextons; in 1824 John succeeded Robert; in 1902 there was another Thomas with his sister Sarah who was sextoness from 1887 to 1910: their mother was sextoness for fifty years before her. The Plants lived in a farm at the end of the Church lane, and the men and women shared the work of the Church.

29 There was a belief in the Glen that left-handedness was a proof of descent from the original Protestant settlers. The Hanbidges at any rate were often left-handed. When I first handled a hay rake in 1882 I held it with my left hand, and my cousins said 'Look! She's a Hanbidge.' A Dublin cousin in 1938 told me he always handled a new tool with his left hand, and his young son uses either hand for writing, like my Father. But I am told that this left-handed theory of descent may have another and an uncomplimentary

origin; for the Irish word for left-handed (ciotagh, kittagh) also means cross, contrary; and another word which means 'on the left' also means 'on the wrong side'.

30 Thompson's Arithmetic made a great impression on him. It was the first intellectual food given to his eager brain. To the end of his life he talked to me about it and thought I would do well to use it.

31 'I made more progress in Scriptural knowledge than I did in its practice. I got my first prayer book in 1822, first Bible next year and my first prize *Sergeant Dale and Little Mary* about the same time.'

32 In 1702 the first legal provision for the relief of the poor in Ireland brought about the establishment of a Foundling Hospital and a Workhouse in James Street in the parish of St James on the south side of the Liffey. By 1730 the building was used exclusively a Foundling Hospital, and a turning wheel or 'foundling cradle' was placed outside the building to receive the babies. Up to 1835 it used to accommodate two thousand deserted children, and five thousand infants were put out to nurse in the country and received in the Hospital when they were old enough. Schoolrooms were provided in the building, boys and girls being taught separately. The Government made an annual grant of from £20,000 to £30,000. The children were placed out as apprentices or servants when old enough, and by 1800 a premium of £10 was given with every boy or girl so placed. Eliza Styles was such an apprentice, employed as a monitor in Donoughmore School, no doubt on Mr. Greene's suggestion. From the beginning the mortality amongst the children was great, and this continued despite the efforts of many good men and women amongst the Governors to improve conditions in the latter part of the eighteenth century. In the early nineteenth century such terrible conditions of dirt, neglect and mortality were revealed that in 1829 the Report of a Select Committee of the House of Commons recommended that no more children should be admitted and that the Hospital should be closed as soon as possible. It was closed in 1839. (From *A Brief History of the Ancient Foundling Hospital of Dublin in the year 1702*, by William Dudley Wodsworth, Assistant Secretary Local Government Board Ireland, 1876.)

33 The Training School in Dublin to which Mr Greene sent my Father was not as I had always supposed the Kildare Place Training School for Teachers, but an institution approximating rather to a secondary school. He entered it at the age of sixteen, being admitted after examination on 19 September 1829. The boys learnt ordinary school subjects and in addition Bell's System of Education. It has proved impossible to trace this school. My Father states that it was held in a house in the premises of the Foundling Hospital and that the Chaplain of the Hospital attended to hear the reports read; but the Protestant Chaplain of the South Dublin Union, which took over the minute books etc. of the Hospital at its dissolution, has no record of this school; and it is not mentioned in the Dublin Directory of 1829 or in any educational report. The Kildare Place Training

School began its work in St James' Parish where the Foundling Hospital stood; and it seems probable that when that school moved to Kildare Place St James' Parish maintained the tradition of such a school, and one was opened in the grounds of the Hospital. Possibly the boys in the school may sometimes have been used as monitors in the Hospital school but my Father knows nothing of this. It is clear that the institution was distinctively Church, as opposed to the undenominational Kildare Place Training School. Bell's System of Education was studied not Lancaster's, both the masters were clergymen, and the Chaplain of the Foundling Hospital attended to hear the reports read.

34 The Rev. James Aiken was born in 1797, and so was in the prime of life when he thundered down the corridor to warn the boys that he was coming, and frightened my poor Father. He was ordained deacon in 1817, married in 1818, and ordained priest in 1820. He was assistant Chaplain of the Magdalen Asylum 1855 to 1865. He died in Dublin in 1871.

35 The lending library would consist of the sets of books issued for that purpose by the Kildare Place Society. Mr Greene used to bring white bread in a basket and give a piece to every boy that had his lesson. Bread was unknown on the farm; there was only oatmeal cake and potato cake.

36 Cf. I Samuel 4: 21.

37 Eleven Irish miles were equal to fourteen English. An Irish acre was about one and five eighths of the English. An Englishman was once heard to lament that he had come to a country where the miles were so long and the pints were so short; really the Irish pint was the same as the English, but I am told that the measures were not always accurate, and perhaps he was unlucky.

38 'Though I could have answered all the questions which the man (he was quite grown up) who sat before me answered.'

39 I still have some of these books. They were Jones on Trinity, Percy's Key to the New Testament, Gisborne's Familiar Survey of the Christian, and a Book on Family Devotion. This last his mother used until she died.

40 I think it must have been at this time that my Father, Vestry Clerk to Donoughmore Parish, was on duty at a wedding when the bridegroom had forgotten the ring. At that time a marriage had to be solemnised before noon, and it was impossible for the groom to get the ring and be back in time; so Mr Radcliffe stopped his watch till the man got back, and it was before noon by the Curate's watch when they were married.

41 He had married Anna Rosetta Hocter in April 1833. He failed to get on through bad debts.

42 Edward Adderley Stopford (1810–74).

43 This school was called Rahan.

44 William and Thomas died very young. My Father was given the name of his dead brother, a custom not uncommon.

45 This crime always lay heavy on his conscience; it was committed on Gibstown Bridge.

46 Kitty was married in 1841. About forty years before consumption was declared infectious my Father maintained that it was so, for his sister caught it from her husband.

47 His brother Edward died in January 1898, not 1899; and Henry in December 1893, not 1894.

48 The River Slaney was a fine trout river, and there were eels there also. Once my grandfather caught an eel in it which was so big that as he carried it home with its head over his shoulder its tail trailed on the ground; and he was a tall man.

49 Since increased.

50 One of her charges had a horrible experience. A fox was doing such damage to the poultry yard that my uncle was driven to dig out his earth; they cut down to it from above, and there they found a duck which had been carried off thirty-six hours before alive, thin and terrified but alive. They brought it home; it drank as if it would never stop; and it was none the worse for its adventure. Many people refuse to believe this story, but it is true; it happened one year while we were in Ireland.

51 While the Royal Irish Constabulary was the national police force, in the capital a separate Dublin Metropolitan Police maintained law and order.

52 This is not quite correct, for the Donoughmore Register gives his baptism as 12 June 1768.

53 Tinnahinch was almost ruined by cattle disease after the Famine. At one time there was only one cow left, a white one.

54 Poors house is an Irish grammatical form of poor house. A free school at the time was sometimes called a poor's school.

55 The door used to be at the lower end of the kitchen by the small bedroom. He could see that it was changed for the full Easter moon was shining.

56 The waking of Protestants still goes on, but it differs from the typical Irish wake. Friends and relatives, both men women, visit the house of mourning for two evenings before the funeral to offer their condolences. They are given tea and something to eat, and stay a short time only.

57 When he came out of Church she did not make room for him beside her on the jaunting car. He told me he did not understand that it was because she was shy.

58 Her grandfather was a sergeant at the siege of Gibraltar.

59 My brother John died 4 January 1919.

60 The only way from Dunedin to Inchclutha then was a rough bush track over a total distance of about seventy miles.

61 The general sense of this passage is clear enough – contrary indications of health/disease in the crop – but the text itself is corrupt. Perhaps we should read *some* for the word *none* (W. J. Mc C.).

62 The Census of 1841 gives the population of Ireland as 8,174,266. In 1841 Stratford had a population of 4,201, and Donoughmore 3,507; but in 1936 Stratford numbered 324 and Donoughmore 307, making with North and South Imaal a total of 780. So the Glen is empty compared with the Glen my Father knew when a boy. In 1882 I saw the ruins of eleven fair-sized houses in a drive of seven miles; and even today you can trace in many places the remains of houses, cabins and tiny hamlets like those of the Flynn weavers.

63 These two sentences constitute the only evidence of Hanbidge's addressing a specific audience in writing his *Memories* – one for whom it was necessary to emphasise the Irish identity of those whose suffering he recalled. Clearly such sentences were not designed for his own family's eyes. (W. J. Mc C.)

64 Hanbidge spells the name of the small seaport Schull as it is pronounced. (W. J. Mc C.)

65 A popular name for the great black petrel or fulmer, generally seen in the Pacific. (W. J. Mc C.)

66 'The cook must have thought I had a big appetite, he cooked every day for me what five or six men ate.'

67 'But did not find them' does not apply to the guineas. My Father's tale runs 'John said he was going again. "I am sure you shall not except over my body." So with a foxy look he took the money out of his pocket and handed it to me. "Now you may go," I said. He had not been gone more than a quarter of an hour when the devil got at my elbow urging me to take it. I wish I had resisted him all my life as well.'

68 A National schoolmaster's pay was then £2 a month with a house and about two acres of land. With this he had to keep himself, his wife, his sister-in-law and six children. They never had meat save when they went to Tinnahinch; and he was up at four in the morning to work his land. He was often too tired to teach properly, he said.

69 She died in the room where his first wife died.

70 The final three words of this sentence do not seem to add to its sense. Hanbidge had been approved in 1857 to join the Mission, and his meaning approximates to *whose tests I had passed in 1857* (W. J. Mc C.).

71 Correctly, Majuba Hill.

72 Matabele Land. There was no news of this expedition for more than six months. (An Englishman, Christopher Bethel, married into the Barolong tribe and fought for them against the Boers in July 1884. Captured, he was tortured to death for the 'crime' of going native. His uncle, Sir Charles Warren, led an expedition to recover the body, a venture which had concealed political and commercial motives (W. J. Mc C.).)

73 My brother, Lieut. Colonel Robert William Hanbidge, died on 8 August 1936 aged eighty-five. He had seen service in three continents and for over fifty-three years, from before the Louis Riel Rebellion in Canada in 1870 until after the Great War. During the War he was Provost Marshal for Tunbridge Wells and district, Camp Commandant at

Brentwood, and Deputy Assistant Adjutant General. He retired in 1920. He told me that Wicklow men from the Crimea, making their way home, used to ask at the schoolmaster's house for food and shelter; and our Father let him, the youngest boy, sit on his knee and listen as they told their tales by the fire; and that made him a soldier. And a generation earlier our grandfather had let his youngest boy, our Father, sit on his knee and listen to the tales of the Wicklow men from Waterloo who sought food and shelter at the farm. My brother said that what our Father repeated to him proved that, tiny child as he was, he really had heard those fireside tales.

74 Both grandsons were born in 1905, not 1906.

75 The London City Mission in Hoxton, an interdenominational Society, was founded on 16 May 1835 by David Nasmith. Its object was 'to extend the knowledge of the Gospel' in the Metropolis, and at first it confined its work to house to house visiting carried on by its missionaries. Gradually its work has developed. First came the introduction of workers specially deputed to visit men; and now there are missionaries to transport workers in their depots, dockers, scavengers, bargees, workers in the great markets, public houses, foreign seamen (European and Oriental) at the docks, etc. There are now two hundred and fifty missionaries; in my Father's time there were more. The house to house visitation is carried on by missionaries who have a local district which belongs to a particular Church or Chapel of the denomination to which the missionary himself belongs, and his work is supervised by his ecclesiastical superior. The personality of the workers is an important factor in the work. How carefully they are chosen the report on my Father shows. It is contained in a Minute of the Committee dated 21 December 1857, and runs as follows –

> The Examining Sub-Committee reported that they had examined Wm. Hanbidge, of Kilranalagh, Baltinglass, Ireland. This candidate is a widower, with 6 children, 2 of whom alone are under our [*sic*] age. He is on the verge of 45 years. He has been a Scripture Reader under the Scripture Readers' Society for Ireland. He is of Protestant parentage. For the last six years he has been employed in teaching a school for the poor. He is an intelligent man, and is straightforward in his replies. His knowledge of Scripture is good. The Sub-Committee think favourably of his general suitability to our work. They recommend that he be sent to the Examiners.
>
> The testimonials of Hanbidge were then read, after which he was called in and examined by the Committee, and on his withdrawal it was agreed that he be sent to the Examiners.' Appointed 28.12.57 Salary £75. There was a small allowance for each child under twelve years.

The Secretary of the Mission, the Rev. W. P. Cartwright, sent me this report, to my surprise and delight, in May 1938. I am very grateful to him. In the covering letter he wrote 'We rarely take men into the Mission who are even 35. So this is a case which shows that may not always be wise.'

My dear Father thought he was a rich man with £75 a year, but he soon found he was not. He was six years in Spitalfields, one year and three months in Whitechapel, eight years and six months in the City and twenty years two months in Hackney. I remember two tales about his work in Spitalfields. The Prince Consort died on Saturday evening 14 December; and the next night, in dead silence, my Father preached in the kitchen of one of the common lodging houses on the text 'A living dog is better than a dead lion.' (Eccl. IX: 4). Once he knocked at the door of a room on the top floor of a tenement house. A very big man opened the door, shouting 'You be off, or I'll throw you downstairs.' Said my Father, buttoning up his coat, 'I don't say you won't but I'll tell you one thing. I shan't go down alone.' Nothing happened.

And in all his work in Spitalfields he was fearless. There were many places in the district where the police dared not penetrate alone, even in daylight; they went in couples. Long Lane, just outside his district where Liverpool Street Station now stands, was a notorious example. But he went everywhere. Drunkenness was rampant. To the end of his life as the Bank Holidays came round he used to continent on the change in the behaviour of the holiday folk, quiet, orderly and respectable, in place of the drunken crowds of the sixties.

It was during his time there that the garrotters, the robbers who strangled, terrorised Whitechapel. He was a strong and a brave man, but he told me that the terror was such that after dark no one ever walked in the shadow of the house but always by the curb. The Bill to give the cat for garrotting was brought in and passed into an Act in a single day (1863), and there was not another case.

As he walked down Whitechapel High Street one day he said to himself 'Hanbidge! Hanbidge! how is it that you are so different at home from what you are in your work?' Many of us know that self-reproach. He speaks of the Irish who lived in Spitalfields in his day. In December 1921 the morning after the Treaty was signed I saw for the first time the new Irish flag; and it was flying from the top window of a house facing Spital Square.

76 My Mother was for some years matron of a reformatory in Birmingham and afterwards of the Trewint Home for Girls in Mare Street, Hackney. They say she had a wonderful way with those girls, who at the very best were difficult and unruly; she loved them and they grew to love her. My brother Robert was about eleven years old when she married our Father, and he told me that she made a happy home out a poor house full of strong wills and undisciplined tempers. Till the end of his life he adored the memory of his stepmother and her sister Annie.

77 The *Monthly Messenger* was a religious magazine of the day.

78 Homerton Training College was opened in 1852 by the Congregational Board of Education as a Training College for men and women teachers in the schools of the Congregational Union and other dissenting bodies. It stood in High Street Homerton and inherited the name and the home of a training college for the Congregational

Ministry, itself the successor of Homerton Academy 'believed to have been the earliest foundation of a collegiate character amongst the Independent Dissenters.' This statement appears in the account of the opening ceremony given in the *Illustrated London News* for 1 May 1852.

Homerton College School which I attended was the practising school for the College students. In 1894 the Congregational Board secured the buildings of Cavendish College, Cambridge, and the College was established there under a new Scheme of the Board of Education as an undenominational training college for women. It is still Homerton College.

79   Edward North Buxton gave these two scholarships, £30 a year for three years. They were formally presented at a meeting of the School Board for London by Sir Charles Reed, the Chairman. My Father was on his holiday at Talbotstown when the letter came that told of my success. They say that he opened it in the yard, and turned to his sister-in-law with a mighty shout 'Martha! She's won! She's won!' This was in the July of 1877. He kept in close touch with his brothers' homes during his life in London, and he took me to Ireland in 1882 for the first time. I remember that as we went a sunset only to be compared with the one he saw in New York was reflected in the canal beside the L.N.W.R., half across England, and when we drove out of Dublin the next morning on the long car beside the Rathmines canal, the long rays of the rising sun had that luminous ethereal quality almost peculiar to Ireland. We had landed at the North Wall at 6 a.m. and went by jaunting car to the starting place of the 'long car', a jaunting car which held six a side, invented by Bianconi an Italian; it went as far as Baltinglass. The next year the railway had been made to Naas, whence we went on by jaunting car. The third year the railway had been finished to Baltinglass.

80   I attended first the Camden School for Girls, then in Camden Road, and afterwards the North London Collegiate School for Girls. These schools are now the two schools of the Frances Mary Buss Foundation.

81   The Cambridge Training College, the first residential Training College for Secondary Teachers in England. Its foundation was due to Miss Buss's initiative.

82   The Cheltenham Ladies College under Miss Beale.

83   The Central Foundation Girls' School, one of the seven schools receiving an endowment from the Estates Governors of Alleyn's College of God's Gift, Dulwich. Founded in 1726 as the St Botolph's Bishopsgate Charity School, it later became the Bishopsgate Ward School.

84   My own dear brother Harry was delicate from his birth. As with his Uncle Robert, love of fishing and neglect of precautions against damp laid the foundation of an early death. He died 24 June 1906. After his death Father Curtis, the astronomer of Stoneyhurst College, wrote to me, 'He was one of the more accurate observers I have known.'

85   Cf. Ephesians 6: 11 (W.J. Mc C.).

A FEW ANECDOTES OF THE IRISH REBELLION OF 1798

1   The famous insurgent leader, Michael Dwyer, working at Ballintruer in the spring of 1798. It is said that he always showed kindness to the Hanbidges.

2   Whatever was the case before, in 1798 practically every small Protestant farmer in the Glen was enrolled in the Yeomanry.

3   Some say a young Hanbidge of Dunlavin helped him to escape. 'He never meddled with politics again till the day he died.' An article in the *Wicklow People* newspaper in 1930 gives a slightly different account of the shooting of the yeomen taken from Prendergast's Sham Squire: 'On the 25th of May, 1798, Captain Saunders of Saunders Grove reviewed his corps of yeomen, and announcing that he had received private information of all those in it who were United Irishmen, ordered all who were such to step from the ranks. Many in the belief that he had true information came forward, and these were immediately pinioned and marched to Dunlavin. On the following day, May 26th, these men with some from another corps, thirty-six in all, were marched to the Fair Green and shot by the Ancient Britons. Only one man, Peter Prendergast, of Bumbo Hall (now Grange Con) who pretended to be dead, escaped. Amongst those shot was John Dwyer of Donard, an uncle of the celebrated Michael Dwyer.'

   Perhaps Captain Saunders made his investigation because his men had shot over the heads of the insurgents as my Father relates.

4   My grandmother was then at Hacketstown. Earlier in the year her husband was with the yeomanry and she was left at Tinnahinch with her two little ones, Betty not three and John a baby in arms. A party of insurgents appeared, killed a sheep and ordered her to roast it and prepare food. When they had eaten they ordered her to kneel and say the 'Hail Mary'. At first she refused, but the serving maid begged her to do so to save the lives of the children and herself; so she did. The men spared her and the house, but they burned the bacon-curing sheds and the pig and drove off the rest of the sheep. The cowhouse at the back of the house today is built on the site of the burnt sheds. (The episode of the besieged house at Hacketstown was rendered memorable in the Victorian consciousness of 1798 through a much reproduced illustration by George Cruikshank in William Hamilton Maxwell's *History of the Irish Rebellion* (1839 and subsequent editions) W. J. Mc C.).

   The official list of persons in the district who suffered losses in 1798 includes: Henry Handbidge [*sic passim*], Kilbelet; John Handbidge, Donoughmore; John Handbidge, Tinnehinch [*sic*]; Mary Handbidge, widow, Merganstown; Robert Handbidge, Holywood. The two Johns are my Father's grandfather and father.

5   'Fire! In the name of God!' she said. This was on June 25th 1798.

6   She pointed over her shoulder to the house and shook her head.

7   The structure and meaning of this sentence are alike unclear: I think Hanbidge means that the retreating rebels took vengeance on fellow United men (from the Glen of Imaal) who, despite their allegiance, had fought against the rebels at Hacketstown (W. J. Mc C.).

8   The route followed by Dwyer's men evidently took in Tinnahinch (Tinnah), the Hanbidges' farm in Donoughmore parish (W. J. Mc C.).

9   Lord Edward was shot just before the rising began. Dwyer maintained his position in the mountains of the Glen until after Emmet's rising in 1803, when he surrendered to Mr Hume. My Father evidently supposed that Mr Hume was murdered on Keadeen Mountain because his promises to Dwyer were not ratified by the Government, but this was not so. It was Mr Hume's father, Captain Hume, who was murdered in October 1798 by a man named John Moore, one of Dwyer's men. According to local tradition he shot Captain Hume on account of a private grudge. He was hanged at Rathdangan, and afterwards gibbeted on the top of Keadeen. The Hume to whom Dwyer surrendered was William Hoare Hume, MP for County Wicklow. Dwyer was joined in Sydney by his young wife, and later became, of all things, a chief constable there. He died in 1815, and his wife over forty years after.

When these notes were just being printed Dr G. [*sic*] Dickson, who is engaged on the first authoritative life of Dwyer, told me that my grandfather's memories of the Rebellion were sometimes incorrect, as follows:

Michael Dwyer left his home and became a captain at the end of 1797, so he must have said 'I work no more' a good while before 26 May 1798, and my grandfather's story ignored the interval.

Captain Michael Dalton was not killed while he was in County Kildare but later, in June 1800, at Moore Park near Castledermot.

Vinegar Hill is close to Enniscorthy some miles from Ferns.

Antrim John, John Mooney, seems to have got mixed up with another man. The Antrim John who deserted from the Antrim Militia in Arklow about the beginning of July 1798 became adjutant to the leader Holt and was shot at Ballyfad Wood early in November that year.

It is easy to understand that with the lapse of twenty years and more before my Father heard his stories my grandfather forgot some details of the events of the Rebellion through which he had lived, especially if they happened outside the Glen.

MATTERS NOT PRINTED IN THE MAIN BODY OF 'MEMORIES'

1   This portion of William Hanbidge's writings, preserved in the four-page Appendix C but not bound into the *Memories* of 1939, is keyed at several points with page references to the printed volume: these indicate that the appendix was printed after the book was finished, though on a number of occasions the significance of cross-reference is obscure. These 'see page 50' etc. headings may break up what was originally a continuous composition by Hanbidge (W. J. Mc C.).

2   Shillelagh is a village to the east of Hacketstown, on the Fitzwilliam estate (W. J. Mc C.).

MARY ANN HANBIDGE'S CONTRIBUTIONS

1   Thomas Francis Greene was the son of William Francis Greene, of Kilranalagh. He became curate at Donoughmore in April 1819, and was regarded as the first clergyman in the area to encourage greater spirituality among parishioners and to take an interest in their material welfare (W. J. Mc C.).